AIRFIX
magazine guide 17

British Tanks of World War 2

Terry Gander and Peter Chamberlain

Patrick Stephens Ltd
in association with Airfix Products Ltd

© Patrick Stephens Ltd 1976

All rights reserved

No part of this publication may be reproduced, stored in a retrieval system or transmitted, in any form or by any means, electronic, mechanical, photocopying, recording or otherwise, without prior permission in writing from Patrick Stephens Ltd

First published — 1976

ISBN 0 85059 232 1

Other Airfix Magazine Guides for military enthusiasts!

No 1 *Plastic Modelling*
by Gerald Scarborough
No 3 *Military Modelling*
by Gerald Scarborough
No 4 *Napoleonic Wargaming*
by Bruce Quarrie
No 5 *Tank & AFV Modelling*
by Gerald Scarborough
No 7 *Warship Modelling*
by Peter Hodges
No 8 *German Tanks of World War 2*
by Terry Gander and Peter Chamberlain
No 9 *Ancient Wargaming*
by Phil Barker
No 12 *Afrika Korps*
by Bruce Quarrie
No 13 *The French Foreign Legion*
by Martin Windrow
No 15 *World War 2 Wargaming*
by Bruce Quarrie

Cover design by Tim McPhee

Text set in 8 on 9 pt Helvetica Medium by Blackfriars Press Limited, Leicester.
Printed on Fineblade cartridge 90 gsm and bound by the Garden City Press, Letchworth, Herts.
Published by Patrick Stephens Limited, Bar Hill, Cambridge, CB3 8EL, in association with Airfix Products Limited, London SW18

Contents

Editor's	introduction	
one	**British tank development up to 1939**	5
two	**British tank development 1939-1945**	10
three	**American tanks in British service**	14
four	**British tank data**	
	The Light Tanks	17
	The Infantry Tanks	20
	The Medium and Cruiser Tanks	31
five	**Data on American tanks in British service**	49
six	**British tank armament**	57
seven	**Camouflage and markings**	59

Editor's introduction

Although there have been dozens of books published on the German tanks of the last war, there have been relatively few on their contemporary British designs, and many people would be hard pressed to name any tanks beyond the famous Sherman (which was American anyway!), Churchill, Crusader and Cromwell. This book helps redress the balance and gives a complete listing of all British tanks used during the last war, together with their main variants and notes on their armament and camouflage schemes, which will be particularly useful to modellers and wargamers.

After two preliminary chapters describing the outline history of British tank development before and during World War 2, and a short note on American tanks in British service, there is a detailed data section which describes each vehicle in chronological order under the three main headings of 'Light', 'Infantry' and 'Medium' or 'Cruiser'. Well illustrated by photographs from Peter Chamberlain's extensive collection, as well as four-view drawings to 1:76 scale of the main types by Gerald Scarborough, this section includes information on the development and active service use of each vehicle, lists its derivatives, such as mine clearing, bridge laying and flame throwing tanks, and finishes with a data table on a representative mark.

Every British tank, from the little Vickers Lights and the airborne Tetrarch, through the Cruiser tanks I to IV, Covenanter, Crusader, Cavalier, Centaur, Cromwell and Comet, and the heavily armoured Infantry Matilda, Valentine and Churchill, is covered in this way.

Chapter five gives similar data on the main American tanks in British service — the Stuart, Lee/Grant and Sherman — although these will be covered in more depth in *Airfix Magazine Guide 26: American Tanks of World War 2*, to be published in 1977.

Finally, there are two chapters on British tank armament, describing not only the 2, 6 and 17 pdr weapons which formed the main weaponry, but also the machine-guns; and on camouflage and markings in the European, North African and Far Eastern theatres.

The amount of information and detail which has been compressed into this book's pages make it an ideal quick reference source for all military enthusiasts, modellers and wargamers, and an especially useful volume for the younger reader who is perhaps unable to afford the more 'glossy' books on the subject.

BRUCE QUARRIE

one

British tank development up to 1939

Although the origins of the tank are shrouded in a mist of conflicting claims and counter-claims, the credit for producing the first design to see combat in large numbers must be given to Great Britain. The arrival of the slow, lumbering tank on the battlefields of France in 1916 and 1917 broke the stalemate that had existed since late 1914 and made possible the mobile, fluid warfare that was to become commonplace between 1939 and 1945. But the tanks of 1916-1918 were slow, unreliable vehicles which were capable of infantry support only, and their basic lozenge design was soon found to be unsuitable for higher speeds than that of a marching soldier. Thus by late 1918 the first light 'Whippet' tanks had been produced and these used a lower track with a superstructure that was to become the 'classic' format for all future tank designs.

After 1918, tank development in Britain came to a very abrupt halt. As the huge armies disbanded in 1919, so did the pool of expertise and experience gained in tank warfare and the voice of the tank protaganists left in the depleted British Army became muted. The Treaty of Versailles seemed at the time to ensure peace in Europe for years to come so the need for expensive arms appeared to be nonexistent, especially for large and expensive armoured fighting vehicles. As a result defence budgets were drastically cut and kept low throughout the 1920s. The promising designs of 1919 and 1920 were abandoned. Thus the Johnson-designed tanks that showed much promise and had some very advanced design features got no further than troop trials in small numbers and eventually found their way to the scrap heap. But one design did emerge in small numbers to enter service with the British Army to replace the 1918 veterans. This was the Vickers Medium Tank Mark 1 which was designed in 1922 and entered service in 1924. It had a turret with a full 360° traverse, sprung suspension which enabled the vehicle to reach higher speeds than had hitherto been possible, and it mounted a useful 3 pdr gun. The Medium series gradually evolved over the years into the Marks 2 and 3 and it was still in use in 1939 and 1940 when it served as a training vehicle and some even saw a small measure of combat in the early desert battles dug-in as pillboxes.

But throughout the 1920s and early 1930s defence budgets remained small and as a result the amount of tank development carried out was limited and often had to be devoted to improving existing equipments rather than producing new designs.* One possible way out of the severe financial restrictions came with the emergence of the Carden-Loyd and Martel designs of the mid-1920s. Both of these designs were for small one or two-man light tanks, or 'tankettes'. Eventually the Carden-Loyd designs became the more successful and were gradually developed into two-man machine-gun carriers. In this form they seemed to provide a form of armoured fighting vehicle that would be available in some numbers as they were cheap, relatively easy to maintain, and relatively easy to produce. These factors of maintenance and production were important factors during the 1920s and 1930s as the peacetime army had few skilled fitters and the peacetime economy was not geared to producing heavy armaments in any numbers. Time was to show that

*Some one-off experimental designs were produced, but none saw service. Some features of these experiments were incorporated into later designs.

Light Tanks Mk VIC of the 8th Armoured Division on manoeuvres somewhere in England, 1941.

Infantry Tank Mk I, Matilda (A II) of the 1st Army Tank Brigade in France, 1940.

the tankette was virtually useless as a battlefield weapon but it did give the British Army a fair measure of valuable experience in the use and handling of mechanised units, and the basic design eventually evolved into the Bren and Universal weapon carriers of World War 2, a development that is outside the scope of this book.

But the Carden-Loyd series did eventually grow in size until a version with a turret emerged. This turret mounted a machine-gun, and from this design, the Carden-Loyd Mark VII, came the origins of what were to be known as the Vickers Light Tanks. These Vickers Light Tanks were produced in some numbers and in a number of Marks and sub-Marks right up until the late 1930s. They grew in weight from the 2½ tons of the Carden-Loyd Mark VII up to the 5.2 tons of the Light Tank Mark V1B in use during World War 2. Like the smaller tankettes, the Light Tanks were relatively inexpensive and could be produced in some numbers. They proved invaluable as policing vehicles in the various trouble spots of the Empire (especially in India) and they

British tanks of World War 2

increased the fund of 'tank knowledge' available to the Army, but as the various design changes were incorporated they became heavier and less reliable. Battle experience in 1940 was to show their light armour and machine-gun armament to make them virtually useless in tank warfare, and they were reduced to the reconnaissance role where they soon proved to be too unreliable and bulky, so eventually they reverted to a training role.

As well as the small fund of mechanical expertise that was gradually accumulated in the 1920s, a great deal of time and attention was devoted to the organisation and control of tanks in battle. One of the tank prophets, Colonel Fuller, put forward the idea of an all-tank force as early as 1918 and during the 1920s experiments were made until in 1927 the Experimental Mechanised Force was formed which was the first all-mechanised formation in service anywhere in the world. It comprised a tank battalion, a tankette and armoured car reconnaissance group and a mechanised machine-gun battalion. This was supported by an artillery regiment that included some early self-propelled guns. The EMF was disbanded in 1928 but it had by then provided a great deal of experience in the tactical handling of mechanised units. Unfortunately some of the lessons 'learned' proved to be incorrect, for one thing that emerged was that the concept of two types of specialised tanks would be needed for the future. Of these, one was to become the 'Cruiser' which would form the main component of the highly mobile armoured formations of the future. The Cruiser tanks were intended to be relatively lightly armoured but fast and possess a good range. The other tank version was the 'Infantry' tank which would be used in support of infantry operations. These tanks had to have thick armour and speed was not essential. In retrospect, it can be seen that this division of the roles of the armoured fighting vehicle was incorrect, especially as British designers continued to neglect the striking power of their progeny and fitted them only with light guns or machine-guns. This neglect of tank armament was to have serious consequences during the early war years. It was thus left to the Germans to put into effect the unheeded gospel of Captain Liddel Hart. This far-sighted philosopher of armoured warfare had correctly foreseen the need for a well-balanced and mobile tank and supporting vehicle formation with good offensive power. His ideas were put to good use by the German Army which produced the panzer divisions that were to be so effective in 1939 and 1940.

But to return to the tank development scene in Britain. The division of the tank into two roles was reflected during the early 1930s when new designs gradually emerged, still under the cloud of severe financial strictures which slowed development not only of the vehicles themselves but also of the production facilities needed to produce large numbers of the eventual designs. As the Infantry or 'I' tanks were fewer in number it is perhaps easier to consider them first. The first 'I' tank to emerge was the A11 which eventually became the Infantry Tank Mark I or Matilda I. There had been various similar designs produced before the Matilda I that would have met the same specification, such as the Vickers Medium Mark III (the 'Sixteen-tonner') and the huge 'Independent' of 1925. Both of these tanks were large vehicles with a number of auxiliary turrets mounting machine-guns. Neither design was accepted for service although a great deal of experimental and trial work was carried out with them. The Matilda I was produced by Vickers in 1936 and the financial strictures then in force showed in the design. Although it was well armoured it had only a machine-gun as the main armament and the basic overall format was simple with no frills. By 1939 it was in service (139 were produced) and it saw action in France in 1940 but by then it had been supplemented by the Infantry Tank Mark II. This was a much more viable

British tank development up to 1939

fighting vehicle which mounted a 2 pdr gun and was very well armoured. Its design work began in 1937 at a time when it had been realised that war was not only likely but imminent and thus more money was available. The Matilda (the II was soon dropped after 1940 when nearly all the Matilda I tanks were left in France) thus emerged as a good design but it was intended for infantry support only and thus lacked speed and mobility, but it was the best of the tanks that went to war with the British Army in 1939. Another 'I' tank was the Valentine, the Infantry Tank Mark III, but whereas the first two Matildas had been produced under government control, the Valentine was a Vickers 'private venture'. Nevertheless, it was ordered off the drawing board in 1938 and the first models appeared in 1940.

The Cruiser tank picture was rather more complex than the 'I' tank programme. In the early 1930s two designs were produced, the A9 and the A10, both of which went into production as the Cruiser Tank Marks I and II. The Mark I had two auxiliary turrets mounting machine-guns, and the suspension was later used on the A10 and Valentine. The Mark II was originally intended to double as an infantry tank and thus had thicker armour, but it was eventually designated a 'Heavy Cruiser Tank'. Both of these early Cruiser tanks were rather unreliable and were never produced in very large numbers (about 200 all told) but they formed a major part of the armoured formations in France in 1940 and took part in many of the desert battle.

In 1936 the tank suspension designed by J. Walter Christie came to the attention of the British War Office who bought one of his vehicles for inspection via Morris Cars Ltd. The design, which incorporated torsion bar suspension and large road wheels, was much in advance of other forms of suspension in use by the British and was already in widespread use on the Russian BT tank series. It was thus decided to incorporate this new Christie suspension into a new Cruiser tank which emerged as the A13 or Cruiser Tank Mark III. A later variant was the Cruiser Tank Mark IV which had a larger turret and more armour. Both were put into widespread production for the increased number of new designs were too many for existing production lines and new lines were set up using heavy industrial companies and railway rolling stock plant.

Much other experimental design work was carried out along with the concentration on production models and one such project was the A14 design which was abandoned in favour of an improved A13 design which became the Cruiser Tank Mark V Covenanter. It was a much lower design than the original and was rather unusual in that most of the design work was carried out by the LMS Railway Company, in itself a reflection of the spread of tank production across British industrial capacity. The haste with which the Covenanter was developed was unfortunately manifested in the general

Cruiser Tank Mk IV (A13 Mk II) vehicles of the 1st Armoured Division.

British tanks of World War 2

Crusader II in service with the Free French during the fighting in the Western Desert, 1942.

unreliability of the vehicle which was continually plagued by mechanical and cooling troubles and the type never saw action, being used for training purposes only.

The basic A13 design was also drawn upon for the Cruiser Tank Mark VI Crusader. This was just beginning to roll off the production lines as the war began and it did not enter service until 1941. In many ways the Crusader can be said to embody much that was wrong with British tank development in 1939 for it contained many of the faults that were to plague the British tank arm throughout the early war years. The division of tank development into the Infantry and Cruiser categories meant that the Crusader, despite having armour thicker than many other British Cruisers, was still too lightly armoured to stand up to German tank and anti-tank guns. Its own 2 pdr armament was too light when opposed to the contemporary German 5 cm and 7.5 cm guns which could both out-range and out-fight the 2 pdr under nearly all conditions. The 2 pdr was also intended as an anti-tank weapon only and thus was unable to fire a useful HE round when called upon to do so. This had led to the development of a 3-inch howitzer which could be mounted on special Close Support or CS tanks. Another trouble of the Crusader in 1939 was that the haste with which it had been produced meant that it had many untried features which proved unreliable and troublesome in service. Many of these troubles were ironed out in time but they affected the Crusader at a time when it mattered most during the Western Desert campaigns of 1941 and 1942.

The above may seem a long list of troubles but in 1939 they were all in the future. Despite its relatively small numbers the British tank arm was well trained and had a long period of gradual and well-instilled tank handling experience. In the Matilda tank it had one of the most powerful and well-armoured fighting vehicles of its day, despite its 2 pdr gun. Tank production lines were set up and vehicles were being produced in large numbers, but battle experience was soon to show that men and materials, however good, were not good enough to stand up to the German method of waging tank warfare.

British tank development up to 1939

9

two

British tank development 1939-1945

The main difficulties experienced by British tank crews in 1939 and 1940 have already been outlined in the last chapter. Unfortunately their difficulties continued in 1941 and 1942. The main reason for this is that tank production lines are both expensive and time-consuming in the amount of effort needed to set up and run. Thus the progeny of the basic A13 design continued in production and service even at a time when harsh experience in the field (and desert) had shown that the basic design was not up to the needs of contemporary warfare. Another problem soon encountered was the need for increasing numbers of tanks in the field to equip Britain's expanding armies and commitments. The events in France in May 1940 meant the loss of over 700 tanks which required a great deal of effort to replace. Many of these tanks were obsolete Light tanks and Cruisers but the remaining armies in Britain and in the Middle East had to have some form of equipment and thus old designs continued in service.

During 1939 and 1940 priority in tank production was given to 'I' tanks. Thus the Matilda II was produced in some numbers and gained a great deal of fame from being the only British tank that could stand up to German tank gun fire in 1940. Its popularity increased during the 1941 campaigns in Africa when it was pitted against the poorly equipped Italian forces, but after that it came up against the more mobile German panzers and its lack of a viable tank gun soon showed it to a disadvantage and it was gradually withdrawn from use, even though it lingered on as a special purpose tank. Another 'I' vehicle that began its service life in late 1940 was the Valentine. This tank was based on the well-proven and tried suspension of the Cruiser Mark II (A10) but had increased armour. The Valentine was destined to continue in production in the UK and Canada until 1944 but after 1941 it was obsolete as its slow speed, and small turret which prevented heavy armament from being installed, did not enable the vehicle to keep pace with requirements. But the Valentine was a good reliable tank that was well liked by its crews. The initial 2 pdr was replaced by a 6 pdr gun and eventually this too was replaced by a 75 mm gun, making the Valentine a viable fighting tank, but this change took place in 1943 at a time when tank armament was well in advance of this increase. Most of the Valentines produced in Canada were sent to Russia and many of the UK Valentines were used in some form or other as special purpose vehicles.

Perhaps the most famous of all the British tanks produced between 1939 and 1945 was the Infantry Tank Mark IV, Churchill (A22). This tank was developed from an earlier trials vehicle, the A20, and the first model was produced in 1940. It was heavily armoured and armed with a 2 pdr gun. In many ways it was a throwback to the tanks of 1918 which it resembled in shape and general appearance. Over a period of years many changes were made to the basic design and heavier armour and armament was added but the general lack of speed and mobility showed it as the anachronism it undoubtedly was, even at the time of its conception. The thick armour of the Churchill often showed to good effect in such campaigns as Tunisia in 1943 but after that date the main use of the Churchill was as the basis for a whole host of special purpose vehicles ranging from bridgelayers through to demolition tanks and flamethrowers.

Despite the general demise of the 'I' tank in battle, the concept took a long

Churchill VI, 75 mm gun in action in Holland 1944. Note track links used for extra protection.

time to die in tank designers' offices. As the war progressed there continued to appear a number of heavy tanks with an 'I' bias, one of which was the Black Prince (A43) which was a developed Churchill with a 17 pdr gun in the turret. The Valiant (A38) was a developed Valentine and the A33 was a heavy assault tank based on the Cromwell. An unlikely design offshoot was the TOG 1 and 2 project which sought to produce an infantry tank using the design team that produced the original tanks of 1916. All these schemes came to nought as far as the troops in the front line were concerned as they all sacrificed mobility for armour protection. Perhaps the most unlikely project was the 73 ton A39 Tortoise which was conceived as a heavy assault tank to breach the expected obstacle of the West Wall during 1944 or 1945. As it turned out the West Wall was breached with unexpected ease and only six trial Tortoise tanks were built after the war was over.

The Cruiser tanks were soon shown to disadvantage in the battles of 1940 and 1941 when their inadequate armament placed them well below parity when they came up against the well armed and mobile PzKpfw III and IV. The immediate solution was to re-arm the Crusaders and Valentines with the new 6 pdr (57 mm) gun in place of the old 2 pdr (40 mm), but as this was happening the Germans were in the process of arming their PzKpfw IVF tanks with the long 7.5 cm gun and the first hint was heard of the Tiger with an 8.8 cm gun. Width restrictions placed on British tank designers meant that the turret rings of British tanks were not wide enough to stand the stresses involved in fitting larger calibre guns and thus new designs were needed to combat the German panzers. The turret ring width thus prevented anything larger than a 2 pdr gun being fitted to the Matilda and the Crusader could accommodate nothing larger than a 6 pdr. Some Valentines and Churchills were fitted with

British tank development 1939-1945

Cruiser Tank Mk VIII, (A27L) Centaur I fitted with 6 pdr gun.

75 mm guns but by that time the need for something heavier still was apparent.

As has already been stated, tank production lines are difficult and expensive to set up and change so the immediate result of the 1941 shortcomings was a series of interim vehicles. These new vehicles were supposed to be produced in two forms. One was as a Cruiser tank and the other as a more heavily armoured 'I' tank. None of the 'I' tank variants saw service but they did consume considerable design and production effort at a time when it could be least afforded.

One of the first of the 'interim' designs was the Cruiser Tank Mark VII, Cavalier (A24). This was a development of the Crusader with a 6 pdr gun and heavier armour but it proved to be a failure and was plagued by a long string of mechanical failures, a poor power-to-weight ratio and a gun that was already obsolescent. As a result the Cavalier was never used in action and was used only for training and such specialised roles as an artillery OP tank or ARV.

Next came the Cruiser Tank Mark VIII Centaur (A27L). This was another interim design pending the emergence of the eventual Cromwell (A27M). The Cromwell depended on the Meteor engine as its power plant (the Meteor was a special version of the famous Rolls-Royce Merlin used to power the immortal Spitfire fighter), but production of this engine was delayed due to the priority given to aircraft needs. Thus the Centaur emerged with the elderly Liberty engine installed but the design was such that the Meteor engine could be retrofitted when available. The initial version was fitted with a 75 mm gun but this version was not to see service as the Centaur was selected for a variety of special roles, one of which was the fitting of a 95 mm howitzer to provide fire support during the 1944 Normandy landings. Other special versions emerged as AA tanks, OP tanks and APCs.

When the Meteor engine did become available it was installed in the Cruiser Tank Mark VIII, Cromwell (A27M). This fast and handy tank mounted a 75 mm gun in its turret which made it one of the more effective of the Cruiser tanks, but by the time it reached service (late 1943-early 1944) it was already outgunned by the long 7.5 cm gun of its adversary the German Panther and well outgunned by the German Tiger. The main drawback of the Cromwell was its width which again prevented the installation of a more powerful gun. Despite this the Cromwell was used extensively in Europe and saw the war out. Production ran to eight marks and a number of special purpose variants were produced.

The need for a heavy gun for tank armament resulted in the selection of the 17 pdr anti-tank gun for tank use. This powerful, heavy gun became the best of all the various guns selected for British tank use and at last put the British tank crews on a parity with their German adversaries. But the new gun needed a new tank design and as a result there was the usual crop of interim designs. Some were fitted as limited-traverse guns to elderly Valentine chassis to produce the Archer. Another interim design was the Cruiser Tank, Challenger (A30). This was intended to be a Centaur/Cromwell chassis with a few changes to accommodate a new turret with the 17 pdr gun but the result was a new design with a longer and wider chassis involving a weight increase and the insertion of an extra road wheel. The overall result was unsatisfactory as the new turret was high and awkward, and to compound these disadvantages the type took a long time to get into production, by which time the Firefly (see next chapter) was in use. However, some Challengers were used in action in 1944 and 1945. Another 17 pdr on a Cromwell chassis was the self-propelled gun, Avenger (A30) which took so long to develop that it did not enter service until the war was over.

The best of all the wartime Cruiser tanks was the Cruiser Tank, Comet (A34). As the war ended it was just entering service in some numbers. On the Comet the vehicle width was not increased but a new form of the 17 pdr was developed with a shorter barrel and breech. This gun was known as the 77 mm and its performance was only marginally inferior to the large 17 pdr, but it could be incorporated in the confines of the Cromwell turret ring. A new turret was designed for the Comet, and the type was in service for many years after 1945.

Another new tank just starting its troop trials as the war ended was the Cruiser Tank, Centurion (A41). This design was intended to end the old Cruiser/Infantry tank categories by combining the attributes of both in one design — in the event the Centurion became a superb Medium Tank of the type preceded by the PzKpfw IV and Panther, but its story is a post-war one and outside the confines of this book.

One odd offshoot of British tank development concerns the Light Tanks. When the last of the Vickers Light tanks passed from use it did not signal the demise of the concept for as early as 1937 a new design, the Light Tank, Mark VII, Tetrarch, was on the Vickers drawing boards. The first was not produced until 1940 when the design was adopted as a possible airborne tank for glider operations, in which role it was used in small numbers in 1944. A later version, the Light Tank, Mark VIII, Harry Hopkins did not see service and neither did its self-propelled gun variant, the Alecto.

British tank development 1939-1945

three

American tanks in British service

Without a doubt, the numbers of tanks produced by British factories alone would never have been able to meet the huge demands made by the British and Commonwealth armies in the field. Despite frantic efforts and enormous diversion of facilities from other war production, the long years of financial stringency from 1920 to 1935 had not enabled the British armament industry to invest sufficient money and plant to meet the tank demands of a long mechanised war. The result, as we have seen in the last chapter, was that the British tank formations were forced into battle in outdated and inadequate vehicles, and the fact that they were eventually able to meet and overcome their German counterparts can be explained by one factor only, and that is the flood of armoured fighting vehicles supplied by the United States of America. The USA became the arsenal of the Allied forces from about 1940 onwards and after their entry into the war in late 1941, supplies of all manner of waepons was given freely and in huge numbers. Britain was one of the main recipients of this huge arms supply, and high on their list of requirements was, not surprisingly, tanks.

The USA supplied three main models of tank to the UK. These three were the Stuart light tank, the Lee/Grant medium, and the Sherman medium. Of these three the most important was the Sherman which was supplied in such numbers that it was in service with the British forces in quantities that outnumbered the total of all other tanks then in use. It was used in all its many and varied forms, but it is not the intention of this book to go into all the various marks and sub-marks of the Sherman family — that will be done in a forthcoming Airfix Magazine Guide. Suffice to say that of all the tanks used by the British forces, the Sherman was qualitatively and quantitatively the most important. Huge numbers were supplied by the USA in the forms of straight sales, Lease-Lend and gifts.

The first American tank to see British service was the Stuart light tank. The first were supplied in July 1941 and were useful light vehicles armed with a 37 mm gun. The design could be traced back to the American M1 which was an American adaptation of a Vickers commercial design (the 'Six-tonner') which had not been adopted by the British Army. It had gradually been developed into the Light Tank M3 and it was this version that became known to the British as the Stuart or (unofficially) the Honey. The Stuart ran to five marks in British use and many were later converted to APCs or command tanks by the removal of the turret.

Perhaps the most important of the early American-supplied tanks was a version of the Medium Tank M3, known to the British as the Grant. This was a 'British' version of the basic M3 with a redesigned turret to accommodate a radio set, but the main reason for its importance was the 75 mm gun mounted in a sponson in the hull. This gun had only a limited traverse but it at last gave the British tank crews a gun that gave them a weapon superiority over the opposing German tanks. Grants first went into action in the desert in May 1942 and gave the German tank crews a nasty shock. The Grant was later supplemented by numbers of the basic unaltered M3 which was known to the British as the Lee. Both types served on throughout the desert campaigns but the sponson-mounted gun often placed the type at a tactical disadvantage and when the Sherman became available the Lee/Grant was withdrawn from use and converted to several special role variants.

14   British tanks of World War 2

General Grant (Medium Tank M3). This vehicle was fitted with a British-designed turret.

The most important American tank in British service was the Sherman, the American Medium Tank M4. The Sherman ran to a huge number of variants with a variety of main armament, ranging from the original turret-mounted 75 mm gun to 76 and 105 mm guns. All these gun variants entered British service at one time or another but the main truly 'British' variant was the Firefly which was the fitting of a 17 pdr gun to the turret of a Sherman IV and VC. In January 1943 the idea of fitting the 17 pdr to a British tank had first been put forward and the result was the Challenger. As a standby design it was suggested that a Sher-

Canadian Ram II 6 pdr gun used for training Canadian armoured units.

man variant be considered and work went on until November 1943. By February 1944 the Challenger programme was in difficulties and thus the Sherman project, by then known as the Firefly, was put into production to take part in the Normandy landings. During and after the Normandy landings, the Firefly was the only tank in British service to have the ability to take on the German Panther and Tiger on anything like equal terms but it was available only in sufficient numbers to be issued at the rate of one per troop, at least initially.

Apart from the Firefly there were numerous other British adaptations of the basic Sherman design but they were all special purpose vehicles. Many British Shermans were equipped with DD (Duplex Drive) 'swimming' gear and were used during the Normandy landings and subsequent river crossings.

Other important American-supplied armoured fighting vehicles were the Priest self-propelled 105 mm howitzer and the Gun Motor Carriage M10. The M10 was an open-topped vehicle with a 3-inch anti-tank gun mounted in a 360° traverse turret on an M4 chassis. In British use it was known as the Wolverine, but many vehicles had the 3-inch gun replaced by a 17 pdr gun when the type then became the Achil-

American tanks in British service

Sherman IVB armed with 105 mm gun (M4A3). The second vehicle is a Sherman IIA (76 mm gun). 8th Army advance on Bologna, Italy, 1945.

les. Another tank supplied to the British was the Light Tank (Airborne) M22, known as the Locust. Some of these light tanks, armed with a 37 mm gun, were used in the airborne operations connected with the Rhine crossings in March 1945.

Although not strictly an American tank, one vehicle that deserves a mention in this chapter is the Canadian Ram. This was a Canadian re-design of the American Medium Tank M3 which featured a 360° traverse turret mounting a 6 pdr gun — originally this was a 2 pdr. The Ram was a remarkable design achievement for the Canadian War Industry which enabled the Canadian armoured units to be equipped with relatively modern tanks and many Ram tanks were sent to the UK to equip Canadian armoured divisions while they were being trained for battle. But the main disadvantage of the Ram was that its turret was too small to accommodate a gun larger than the 6 pdr, and when sufficient M4 tanks became available the Ram was withdrawn from service and thus never did see action as a tank.

But the Ram did see extensive action as a special purpose vehicle. It was used as an OP tank and as an ARV. It was used as an APC by the simple expedient of removing the turret and in this form it was used as the Kangaroo troop carrier. There were several experimental versions but the most important was the Sexton self-propelled gun. This was a major open-topped redesign of the basic Ram chassis to mount a 25 pdr gun-howitzer, and by the end of the war 2,150 had been built to equip Canadian and British artillery units in armoured divisions. The Sexton was a successful and well-liked vehicle and remained in service with the British Army until the late 1950s and is still in use with some countries today in 1976.

four

British tank data

The Light Tanks

The Vickers Light Tanks were a progressive development of the Carden-Loyd and Martel tankettes — indeed the Light Tank Mark I was the production version of the Carden-Loyd Mark VIII. It appeared in 1929 and was built by Vickers-Armstrong as were nearly all the subsequent Light Tanks. In 1930 the Mark I was superseded by the Mark II (very few Mark Is were built) and in this form became the true prototype of the later Marks. It had a two-man crew, armament was a .303 machine-gun, and the Horstman suspension first used on the Mark I continued in use in a strengthened form. The Mark II was soon replaced in production by the Marks IIA and B which differed in detail only, and a special Mark IIB was built for service in India where they were used on the North-West Frontier. The next production version was the Mark III which was sent to equip a tank battalion in Egypt. On this Mark the centre of gravity was moved to the rear and the suspension was further modified.

With the Mark IV came a more drastic revision of the original design. Production methods were altered so that

Right Light Tank Mk IV used for training on Salisbury Plain, 1940. **Below** Light Tank Mk VIB on reconnaissance in the Western Desert, 1940. Note the recognition white/red/white stripes painted on side of turret.

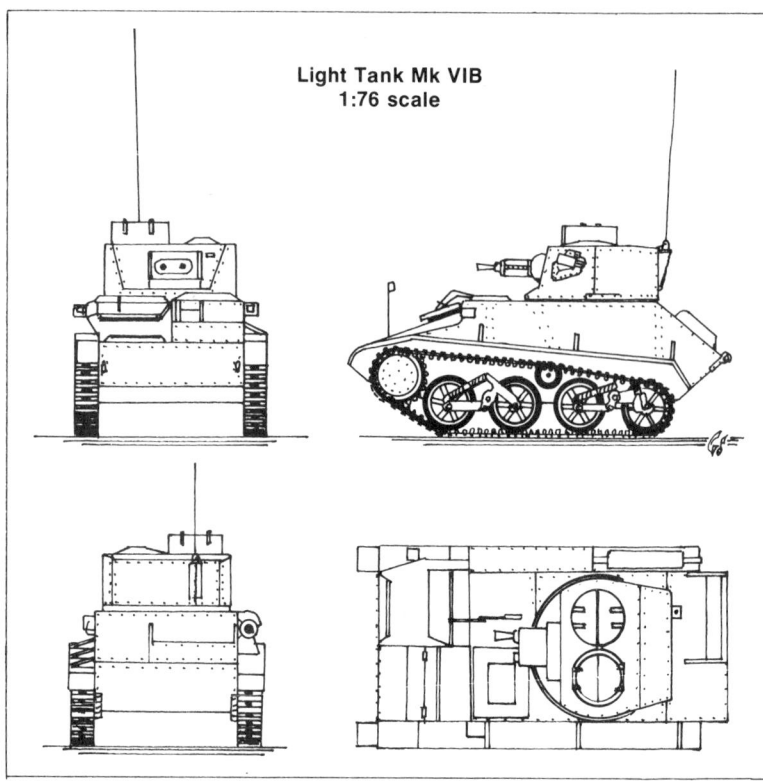

Light Tank Mk VIB
1:76 scale

the hull itself now became the chassis instead of the previous practice of armour being hung on a chassis separate from the hull. The new structure was stronger and lighter. At the same time the turret position was placed higher and the rear idler wheel was omitted. Some vehicles mounted a .5-inch machine-gun instead of the more usual .303, but the Mark IV was not a very successful variant as it was too high for its length and thus had a poor cross-country performance.

The next Mark was the Mark V which was the first to use a two-man turret and the armament was increased to one .5-inch machine-gun and one .303-inch machine-gun. To accommodate the extra crew member the hull was enlarged slightly which had the advantage of improving the cross-country performance. By this time, 1935, the British Army had gained considerable light tank experience and the lessons learned were incorporated into the Mark VI, after only a few Mark Vs were built.

The Light Tank Mark VI was produced in 1936 and featured an enlarged turret to house a new wireless set. Armour thickness varied from 4 to 15 mm and the weight rose from the 4.15 tons of the Mark V to nearly 5 tons. The Mark VI was soon followed by the Mark VIA with a slightly revised suspension and a revised cupola for the commander. But it was the Mark VIB which was produced in larger numbers than any other of the Light Tanks, and numerically, it formed the bulk of the vehicles used in France in 1940 and in the early desert battles. In action, its machine-gun armament was found to be practically useless when opposed by almost any enemy tank and the light armour was soon

Light Tank Mk VII, Tetrarch.

found to be far too thin. In fairness to the design it should be stated that the Light Tank was intended only as a reconnaissance vehicle but the lack of modern battle tanks in service with the British Army forced their use in a role for which they were unsuited. Losses in France and North Africa were heavy and as soon as Stuart tanks became available in 1941 the Light Tanks were replaced and thereafter were used only as training vehicles.

There was one further Light Tank Mark, the Mark VIC. This had broader wheels and tracks, a revised turret with no cupola, but the main change was to the armament. Up till the Mark VIC, all the Light Tanks used either .303 or .5-inch Vickers water-cooled machine-guns which were modified for tank use by the addition of pistol grips and water-circulation systems. These bulky guns were changed by the introduction of 7.92 and 15 mm Besa machine-guns, both air-cooled weapons of Czech origin.

But although the Light Tank disappeared from the tank parks of the British Army after 1941, another light Vickers design remained. This was the Light Tank Mark VII, the Tetrarch, which was first designed in 1938. It was produced in relatively small numbers but was used in action in Madagascar in 1942. Thereafter it was used as a glider-borne tank and saw action in this role in Normandy in 1944 and at the Rhine crossings in 1945. It was flown into action by the Hamilcar glider which was designed specifically for the Tetrarch. The Tetrarch had a different suspension than the earlier Light Tanks and mounted a 2 pdr gun, but some vehicles mounted a 3-inch howitzer as close support weapons (the Tetrarch 1CS). Some Tetrarchs were used to test early DD (Duplex-Drive) flotation gear, and some were sent to Russia. A further Mark, the Mark VIII, Harry Hopkins, did not see service and neither did a self-propelled gun version, the Alecto.

Data Light Tank Mark VIB

Weight	4,903 kg/10,800 lb
Maximum road speed	56 kph/35 mph
Maximum cross-country speed	40 kph/25 mph
Road range	209 km/130 miles
Length	3,950 mm/155.5 inches
Width	2,057 mm/81 inches
Height	2,222.5 mm/87.5 inches
Engine horse power	88
Track width	241 mm/9.5 inches
Wheel base	1,740 mm/68.5 inches
Armament	1 × .5-inch machine-gun
	1 × .303-inch machine-gun
Armour thickness	4 to 14 mm/0.1575 to 0.55 inch
Crew	3

Data Light Tank Mark VII Tetrarch

Weight in action	2,627 kg/16,800 lb
Maximum road speed	64 kph/40 mph

British tank data

Data Light Tank Mark VII Tetrarch continued

Maximum cross-country speed	45 kph/28 mph
Road range	225 km/140 miles
Length overall	4,305 mm/169.5 inches
Width	2,311 mm/91 inches
Height	2,121 mm/83.5 inches
Engine horse power	165
Track width	241 mm/9.5 inches
Wheel base	1,981 mm/78 inches
Armament	1 × 2 pdr (some fitted with Littlejohn Adaptor)
	1 × 7.92 mm MG
Ammunition carried	50 × 2 pdr
	2,025 × 7.92 mm
Front armour	6-10 mm/0.24-0.39 inch
Side armour	6 mm/0.24 inch
Roof armour	4 mm/0.16 inch
Floor armour	14 mm/0.55 inch
Crew	3

The infantry tanks

Infantry Tank Mark I, Matilda (A11)

The design of the Infantry Tank Mark I began in 1934 and the prototype was delivered in 1936. By 1940 139 had been built. The design was a very simple, rugged two-man vehicle with thick armour but the main armament was only a machine-gun. It was intended that the small 'Matilda' (as it was soon nicknamed) would operate at the walking pace of the infantry it was intended to support, and in France in 1940 it proved to be an unsatisfactory vehicle and many were left behind after Dunkirk. Those remaining after 1940 were used for training purposes only, but before that, in 1939, one Matilda was used in early mine-clearing experiments.

Infantry Tank, Mark II, Matilda II (A12)

The first Mark II Infantry Tank was delivered in 1938, and its design was entirely new and owed nothing to that

Data Matilda I

Weight in action	11,186 kg/24,640 lb
Maximum road speed	12.8 kph/8 mph
Maximum cross-country speed	9 kph/5.6 mph
Road range	129 km/80 miles
Length	4,851 mm/191 inches
Width	2,286 mm/90 inches
Height	1,867 mm/73.5 inches
Engine horse power	70
Track width	292 mm/11.5 inches
Wheel base	1,930 mm/76 inches
Armament	1 × .5-inch MG or 1 × .303-inch MG
Ammunition carried	4,000 rounds
Front armour	65 mm/2.56 inch
Side armour	60 mm/2.36 inch
Rear armour	50 mm/1.97 inch
Roof armour	12 mm/0.47 inch
Crew	2

Above *Matilda II in action in the Tobruk area.* **Right** *Infantry Tank Mk II, Matilda (A12). This vehicle is a Matilda I captured by the Germans during the fighting in France, 1940.*

of the Mark I. It had its origins in 1936, but early production was slow and by 1940 only a few units in France had been issued with them. The Matilda II was the most powerful tank available to the British forces in 1939 and 1940 as it was a modern, well-armoured design but it lacked hitting power due to the 2 pdr gun installed. It was also difficult to produce due to its complex design, but when production ended in 1943, 2,987 had been produced. The thick armour of the Matilda II was one of its most valuable assets, and in France and the early desert battles it was proof against all German anti-tank guns other than the infamous '88'. But the Matilda (the II was dropped after 1940 when the Matilda was withdrawn) lacked speed and the small turret ring prevented anything heavier than the 2 pdr being fitted so after 1942 the Matilda was used for a whole host of special purposes. The Matilda did remain in use in the Far East until 1945 with the Australian Army and some Matildas were supplied to Russia. The full range of Matilda variants is mentioned below:

Infantry Tank Mark II. First production type.
Infantry Tank Mark IIA. The Mark II fitted with a 7.92 mm Besa MG.
Infantry Tank Mark IIA*. AEC diesel engines replaced by Leyland engines. Known as Matilda III.
Matilda IIICS. Fitted with 3-inch howitzer in place of 2 pdr.
Matilda IV. Infantry Tank Mark IIA**. Improved Leyland engines.
Matilda V. As Mark IV with gear improvements.
Matilda CDL. These were Matilda IIs and Vs fitted with a new turret which contained a powerful searchlight for illuminating night battlefields. (CDL — canal defence light, a 'cover' name). Never used in action.
Baron. This was a turretless Matilda hull fitted with a mine 'flail' for mine clearing. The Marks I and II retained the turret — the Mark III had engines

British tank data

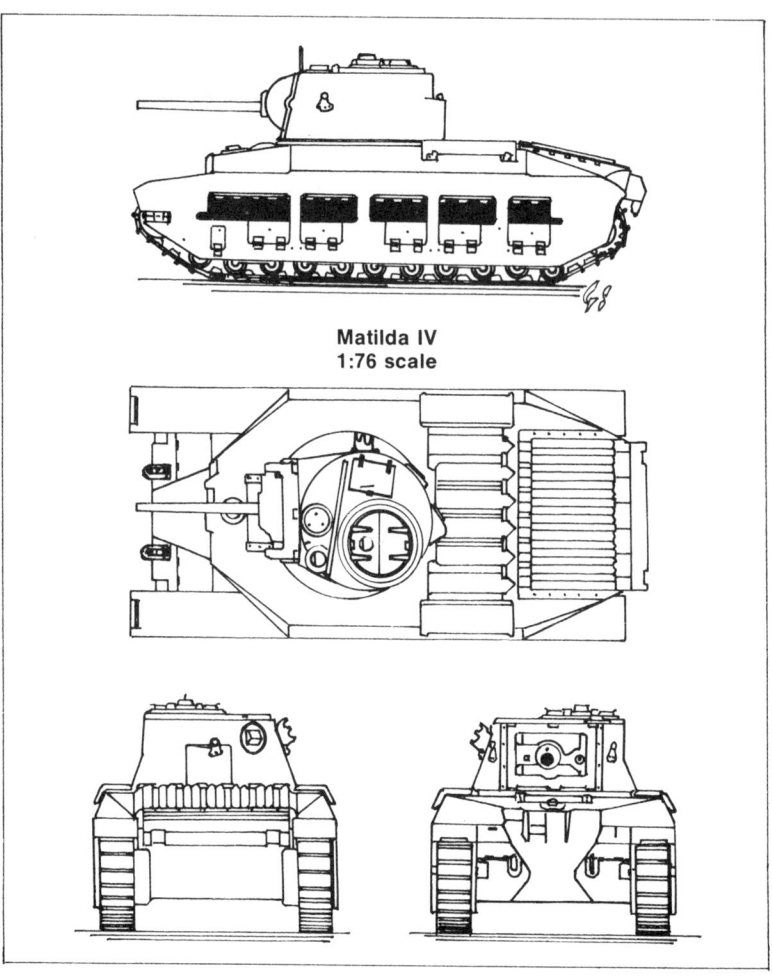

Matilda IV
1:76 scale

for turning the flails mounted on the sides.

Matilda Scorpion. A Middle East mine clearing flail tank — used at El Alamein in 1942.

Matilda with AMBA. On the mine-clearing variant, the Matilda pushed heavy rollers.

Matilda with Carrot. Carrot was a 600 lb/272 kg demolition charge held on a frame in front of the Matilda. It was placed against an obstacle and detonated from inside the tank.

Matilda Frog. An Australian flamethrower installed in place of the gun.

Matilda Murray. Another, later, Australian flamethrower.

Matilda Dozer. An Australian Matilda fitted with a bulldozer blade for obstacle clearing.

Matilda with Inglis Bridge or Trench Crossing Device. Two 'pushed' bridges for crossing gaps or trenches.

Matilda with Crane. A steel bipod mounted on the front of a Matilda used for fitting CDL turrets.

Infanterie Panzerkampfwagen Mark II 748 (e). A captured Matilda as used by the Germans.

22   British tanks of World War 2

Above *Matilda Scorpion, Mine Flail tank operating in the advance at El Alamein, 1942.* **Right** *Matilda III CS. Armed with a 3-inch howitzer as a close-support tank. The clenched mailed gauntlet painted on the front of the vehicle is the badge of the 6th Armoured Division.*

Data (Matilda III)

Weight in action	26,950 kg/59,360 lb
Maximum road speed	24 kph/15 mph
Maximum cross-country speed	12.8 kph/8 mph
Road range	257 km/160 miles
Length	5,613 mm/221 inches
Width	2,591 mm/102 inches
Height	2,515 mm/99 inches
Engine horse power (Marks I-II)	2 × 87 hp (AEC)
Engine horse power (Marks III-V)	2 × 95 hp (Leyland)
Track width	355 mm/14 inches
Wheel base	2,070 mm/81.5 inches
Armament	1 × 2 pdr (or 3-inch howitzer on CS)
	1 × 7.92 mm MG
Ammunition carried	92 × 2 pdr
	2,925 × 7.92 mm
Front armour	78 mm/3 inch
Side armour	75 mm/2.95 inch
Rear armour	55 mm/2.16 inch
Turret armour	75 mm/2.95 inch
Crew	4

Infantry Tank, Mark III, Valentine

The Valentine was originally a Vickers private venture based on the considerable fund of experience gained with the A9 and A10 Cruiser tanks, and used the same suspension and many other components. In 1939 it was thus possible to order the Valen-

British tank data 23

tine infantry tank almost 'off the drawing board' and as a result of the development carried out on the earlier, lighter tanks, the Valentine was a reliable and useful vehicle. The first Valentines entered service in 1940 and for a while they were used as Cruiser tanks as a result of the prevalent tank 'famine' experienced until late 1941, and in the desert campaigns they proved to be good fighting vehicles, although they were hampered by the 2 pdr armament and the vehicle's lack of speed. In time the 2 pdr was replaced by a 6 pdr gun and eventually by a 75 mm gun, but these changes are covered below. The Valentine was one of the most widely produced of all British tanks (by early 1944 when production ceased 8,275 had been built) but after 1943 its value as a fighting tank declined and the type was used as the basis for a long string of special-purpose vehicles. The Canadians also opened a production line and built 1,420 vehicles nearly all of which were sent to Russia.

Valentine I. Original production version with 135 hp petrol engine and 2 pdr gun.

Valentine II. Fitted with 131 hp diesel engine — some fitted with desert sand shields and long-range external tanks.

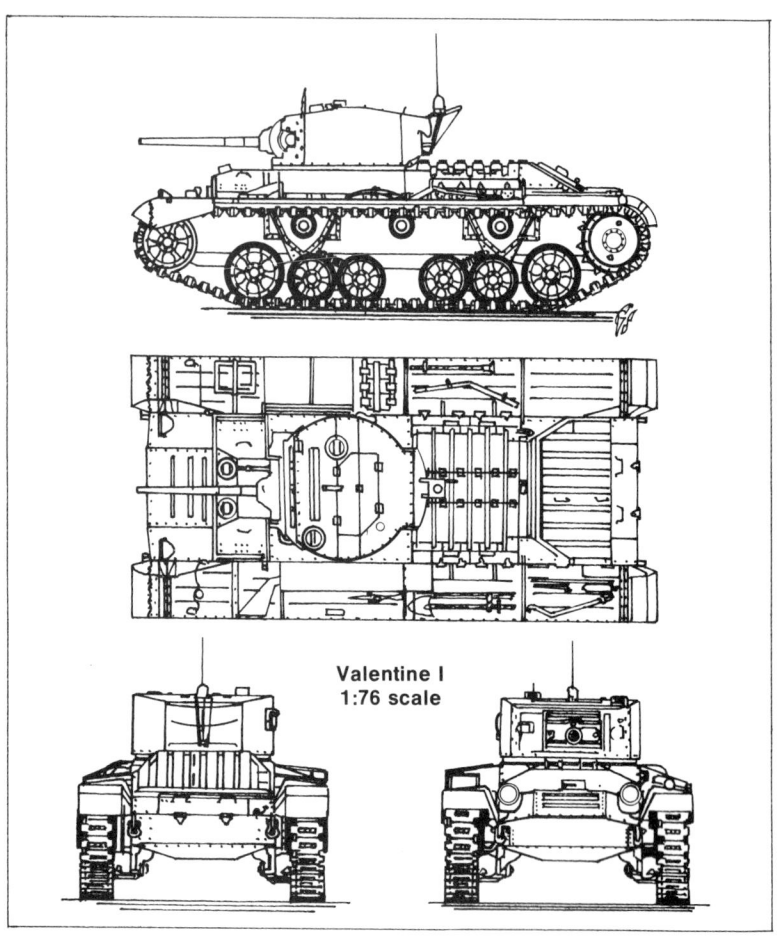

Valentine I
1:76 scale

British tanks of World War 2

Valentine III. Enlarged turret to accommodate extra crew member.
Valentine IV. New 138 hp diesel engine in Valentine II.
Valentine V. New diesel engine in Valentine III.
Valentine VI. First Canadian production version, similar to Valentine IV.
Valentine VII. Improved Valentine VI with detail changes.
Valentine VIII. Upgraded version with 6 pdr gun — turret crew reduced to two. Conversion from Valentine III.
Valentine IX. Conversion from Valentine V with 6 pdr gun.
Valentine X. 1943 production version with 6 pdr gun and new 165 hp diesel engine.
Valentine XI. As Valentine X but with 75 mm main armament — final production version.

Self-propelled Gun, Bishop. The Bishop was an attempt to provide some form of SP gun support to the British armoured divisions. It housed a 25 pdr gun in an armoured box mounted on a Valentine chassis. The Bishop was not a great success and was replaced by the M7 Priest 105 mm gun as soon as possible. About 80 were produced but after 1943 they were withdrawn.

Self-propelled Gun, Archer. Unlike

Above *Valentine I of the 11th Armoured Division on exercise in the Northern Command, 1941.* **Below** *Valentine III, note auxiliary fuel tank.*

British tank data 25

the Bishop, the Archer was a much more successful conversion of the basic Valentine which mounted a 17 pdr A/T gun pointing to the rear on a limited-traverse mounting. It was used as a 'tank-killer' from late 1944 onwards, and proved a popular and useful weapon.
Infantry Tank, Valiant (A38). This was a 1944 improvement of the basic Valentine design but only prototypes were built as by 1945 there was no further need for an infantry-type tank.
Valentine CDL. This mounted the same CDL turret as the Matilda CDL but was not used in action.

in Burma 1944.
Valentine 7.92-inch Flame Mortar. Heavy mortar mounted in turretless Valentine. Trials only.
Valentine with 6 pdr anti-tank mounting. Trials vehicle with 6 pdr on open mounting, 1942.
Valentine DD. At one time it was decided that the Valentine should be the standard 'swimming' tank but in 1944 this role was taken over by the M4 Sherman and the Valentine DD was used for trials and training only.
Valentine Flamethrowers. Various trial machines that were used to develop flame warfare devices.

Data Valentine II

Weight in action	17,700 kg/39,000 lb
Maximum road speed	24 kph/15 mph
Maximum cross-country speed	12.8 kph/8 mph
Road range	145 km/90 miles
Length	5,410 mm/213 inches
Height	2,273 mm/89.5 inches
Width	2,629 mm/103.5 inches
Engine horse power	131
Track width	355 mm/14 inches
Wheel base	2,210 mm/85 inches
Armament	1 × 2 pdr
	1 × 7.92 mm Besa MG (co-axial)
	1 × .303-inch Bren MG
	1 × 2-inch smoke discharger
Ammunition carried	60 × 2 pdr
	3,150 × 7.92 mm
	600 × .303-inch
	18 × 2-inch smoke bombs
Front armour	60 mm/2.36 inch
Side armour	60 mm/2.36 inch
Turret front armour	65 mm/2.56 inch
Crew	3

Valentine OP/Command. This was a Valentine with the main gun removed to provide space for wireless sets, map boards, etc. Used in Archer formations.
Valentine Scorpion II. Mine clearing flail tank — not used in action.
Valentine AMRA Mark Ib. Mine roller device not used operationally.
Valentine Snake. Mine clearing device dragged across a minefield. Actually a pipe filled with explosive to blow a passage across a minefield.
Valentine Bridgelayer. Some used

Infantry Tank, Mark IV, Churchill (A22)

The War Office planners of 1939 foresaw a European campaign that would be fought under the same static conditions that prevailed in 1914-1918, and accordingly thought in terms of trench-crossing, obstacle-crossing abilities and the ability to survive continued artillery bombardment when thought was given to ordering a new Infantry Support tank. Their initial requirements went as far as envisaging a return to the 'lozenge' shape of the first World War I tanks but in 1939 a requirement was issued for a heavily armoured tank with 'all-round' tracks for wide trench crossings. This was built as the A20 and it was not a success due to many inherent design faults and the project was handed over to Vauxhalls who carried out a major redesign at a very fast pace to produce a new prototype known as the A22. This hurried redesign was carried out in a year and as a result the A22 design, soon ordered as the Infantry Tank Mark IV and christened 'Churchill', displayed a wide range of 'snags' that manifested themselves in general unreliability and numerous breakdowns. These faults were gradually eliminated but the result was that many of the early production tanks had to be returned to the factories or workshops for major 're-work' programmes.

The first Churchills were produced in mid-1941 at a time when there were very few British tanks available and as a result production was rapid and the numbers involved were large. Vaux-halls became the parent company to a whole host of shadow factories and concerns which produced the large number of components needed for the Churchill. Throughout its service life the basic design underwent a multitude of changes, not only to such major items as the engines but also to such details as internal stowage bins and wiring. For the man in the field the most important changes were to the armament. The first Mark had a 2 pdr gun in the turret and a 3-inch howitzer in the nose but later Marks had the howitzer replaced by a machine-gun. The 2 pdr was eventually replaced by a

Above right *Self-propelled 17 pdr gun, Archer. Rear view of the 17 pdr anti-tank gun mounted on the chassis of the Valentine.* **Right** *Churchill II on manoeuvres.* **Below** *Churchill IV, 6 pdr gun in cast turret.*

British tank data

6 pdr turret gun and the later Marks used a 75 mm gun. As the number of Marks were produced there were numerous retrofit programmes so that early Marks were bought up to later standards and there were numerous 'mongrel' Marks in service — this should be borne in mind when using the tables below.

In service the Churchill proved itself a good, well armoured Infantry tank. In the desert its slow speed was a disadvantage but in the Tunisian mountains and the Italian terrain it proved invaluable to the extent that it remained in production at a time when it had been thought its useful life as a design would be over. Thus, in Normandy in 1944 the Churchill was the most numerous British tank in use and it remained in action until the war ended.

Perhaps the Churchill's main contribution to the war effort was not as a gun tank but as the basis for a very wide range of special purpose tanks. The Churchill became the basis of tanks used as flamethrowers, bridges, AVREs, demolition vehicles, mine-clearers and mobile cranes. There were so many of these variants that the listing below can only mention the most important of them.

Churchill I. 1941, the first production model with 2 pdr turret gun and hull-mounted 3-inch howitzer. No track guards.

Churchill II. As Churchill I but with 3-inch howitzer replaced by machine-gun.

Churchill IICS. As Churchill I but with turret gun replaced by 3-inch howitzer and 2 pdr in hull. Few produced.

Churchill III. A major redesign with a 6 pdr turret gun, track covers, new engine intake arrangements and general strengthening and detail changes. Main visual change was an enlarged turret.

Churchill IV. As Churchill III but with cast turret in place of the welded version on the III.

Churchill IV (NA75). Mediterranean theatre conversion of Churchill IV to take an American 75 mm gun. Used until 1945 in Sicily and Italy.

Churchill V. As Churchill IV but armed with a 95 mm howitzer for close support role.

Churchill VI. Interim conversion pending the Churchill VII.

Churchill VII. (A22P). A major redesign, this version had a British 75 mm gun mounted in an enlarged turret, thicker armour, a new gearbox and many other detail changes. In service until 1945.

Churchill VIII. As Churchill VII but mounting a 95 mm howitzer.

Churchill IX. Churchill III or IV reworked to Churchill VII standard but retaining the 6 pdr gun.

Churchill X. Churchill VI reworked as Churchill IX but with 75 mm gun.

Churchill X LT. Reworked Churchill VI with original turret.

Churchill XI. Churchill V with new turret and extra armour.

Churchill XI LT. Reworked Churchill V with original turret.

Gun Carrier, 3-inch, Mark I, Churchill. In late 1941 the idea of mounting surplus 3-inch AA gun barrels on to Churchill tanks was proposed, but production was slow and the whole project came to nought after a few conversions had been made. The gun was mounted in a limited-traverse fixed turret and could have been a viable 'tank-killing' weapon but none saw action.

Infantry Tank, Black Prince (A43). A new design based on the Churchill but mounting a 17 pdr gun in a new turret on a widened hull. Not produced until May 1945 and not taken into service.

Specialised versions

The AVRE. (Armoured Vehicle, Royal Engineers). This was a version produced for use by sappers when attacking heavily defended targets such as protected beaches or strongpoints. The turret mounted a device known as a Petard mortar which fired demolition charges, and the vehicle could carry fascines and such other specialised equipment such as assault bridges, mat-laying devices for crossing soft ground or wire obstacles,

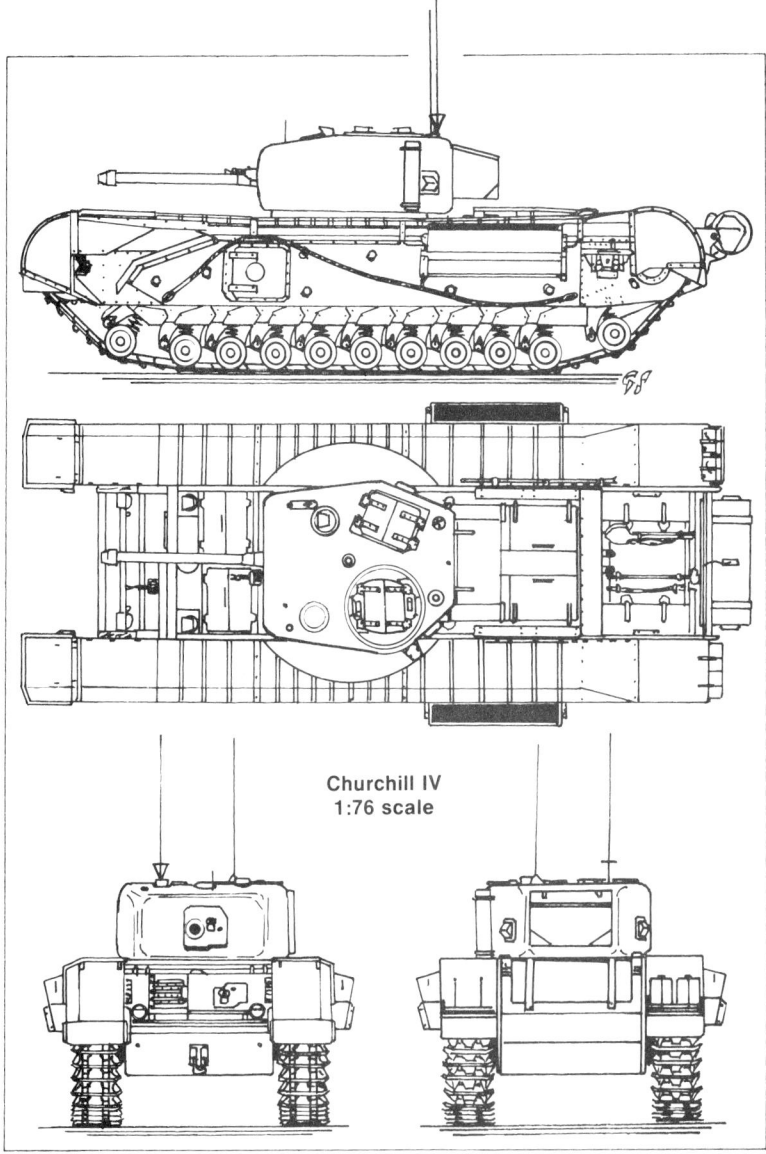

Churchill IV
1:76 scale

and mine-clearing ploughs or rollers.
The ARV. (Armoured Recovery Vehicle). There were two main Marks of ARV with a specialised BARV for use on beaches. The ARVs carried jibs and winches to assist stranded tanks or other vehicles.
Bridging vehicles. There were many of these, not all of which saw action. The Arks used the turretless tank hull and track as part of the bridge while most others actually carried the bridge into position, laid it and then withdrew. Variants were Churchill Ark Mark I; Churchill Ark Mark II (two patterns, the UK and Italian); Churchill Bridgelayer; Churchill Octopus; Churchill GE Ramp (Great Eastern); Lake-

man Ark; and Woodlark.

In addition to the above the Churchill or Churchill AVRE was often used to push into position Bailey bridges which were assembled on to tracked carriers. This system was used in Italy and elsewhere.

Flamethrowers. Three main versions: Oke — used at Dieppe to no avail; Crocodile — the main version. Fuel for the hull-mounted projector was carried in a two-wheeled trailer; and Cobra — experimental only.

Mine ploughs. These were devices usually fitted to AVREs — not all saw service. Plough A to D; Harrow; Bullshorn Plough; Jeffries Plough; Farmer Front; Farmer Track; and Farmer Deck.

Mine-clearing devices. These mainly consisted of rollers pushed ahead of the tank. Churchill with AMRA Mark IIe; Churchill with AMRCR; and Churchill with CIRD — various sizes of wheels.

Demolition devices. These usually consisted of metal frames held in front of the tank to which demolition charges could be attached. In action the Churchill ran up to the strongpoint target, placed the charge (which could be detached) and the demolition charge was then exploded. Versions were: Light Carrot; Heavy Carrot; Jones Onion; Quinson Device; Goat Mark III; Elevateable Goat; and Bangalore Torpedo.

Other variants. Ardeer Aggie — an experimental AVRE with a larger Petard mortar; Snake — Minefield clearing version using Gun Carrier chassis; Woodpecker — AVRE with four Petard mortars; and Conger — Variation of Snake.

In addition to all the above variants there were many other post-war conversions which are outside the scope of this book.

Data Churchill IV

Weight in action	39,661 kg/87,360 lb
Maximum road speed	24.9 kph/15.5 mph
Maximum cross-country speed	12.8 kph/8 mph
Road range	145 km/90 miles
Length	7.442 mm/293 inches
Width	2,743 mm/108 inches
Height	3,251 mm/128 inches
Engine horse power	350
Track width	355 mm/14 inches

Churchill V armed with 95 mm howitzer advances into Germany 1945.

British tanks of World War 2

Data Churchill IV continued

Wheel base	3,810 mm/150 inches
Armament	1 × 6 pdr Mark 3 or 5
	2 × 7.92 mm MG
	1 × 2-in smoke projector
	1 × .303-inch Bren LMG
Ammunition carried	84 × 6 pdr
	6,975 × 7.92 mm
	30 × 2-inch smoke bombs
	600 × .303-inch
Front armour	101 mm/3.98 inch
Side armour	76 mm/ 3 inch
Rear armour	50 mm/1.97 inch
Turret front armour	89 mm/3.5 inch
Crew	5

Churchill Crocodile flame throwers and British troops enter the German town of Hongen, 1945. The Crocodiles are painted white for snow camouflage.

The Medium and Cruiser tanks

Medium Tanks Marks II, IIA, II* and II**

The Vickers Medium Tank was produced in the late 1920s and, with the earlier Mark I, formed the main bulk of the Royal Tank Corps up to 1938. During this period a number of these machines were modified and armed with Vickers machine-guns, replacing the Hotchkiss guns.

The Medium Mark II was completely obsolete by the start of World War 2 and was used for training, though some that were based in Egypt were used in the early desert battles.

After the loss of most of Britain's front line tanks in the withdrawal from France these Medium Tanks were pressed into service as battle tanks for Home Defence.

British tank data

Top *Churchill ARK Mk II (UK Pattern). The vehicle was driven into ditch, river or gap that was required to be bridged, and the ramps were dropped.* **Above** *Churchill Bridgelayer moving up to the Antwerp-Turnhout Canal 1944. An arm worked by hydraulic pressure lifted the bridge and deposited it across the gap to be bridged.*

Top *Churchill IV (NA 75) advances on to the river Po, Italy, 1945.* **Above** *Medium Tank Mk II** captured by the Germans during the early campaign in the desert.*

Data Medium Tank Mark II**

Weight in action	13,729 kg/30,240 lb
Maximum road speed	29 kph/18 mph
Maximum cross-country speed	16 kph/10 mph
Road range	193 km/120 miles
Length	5,334 mm/210 inches
Width	2,781 mm/109.5 inches
Height	3,010 mm/118.5 inches
Engine horse power	90
Track width	330 mm/13 inches
Wheel base	2,591 mm/102 inches
Armament	1 × 3 pdr
	3 × 0.303-inch MG
Armour (overall)	8 mm/0.315 inch
Crew	5

Cruiser Tank Mark I (A9)

The A9 design was originally designated a Medium Tank when it was first designed by Vickers in 1934. The polarisation of Army thought into Cruiser and Infantry tank definitions turned the A9 into the Cruiser Tank Mark I, of which a total of 125 were built. The Cruiser Mark I saw some action in France in 1940 and again during the early desert battles but in service it proved to be too slow and too lightly armoured. One of its best design features was its suspension which was later adopted for the Valentine Infantry tank. The main armament of the Cruiser Mark I was the 2 pdr but some tanks carried a 3.7-inch howitzer for close support work and in this form they were known as the Cruiser Tank Mark ICS.

Cruiser Tank Mk I (A9) of the 7th Armoured Division, Western Desert, 1940.

Data Cruiser Tank Mark I

Weight in action	13,042 kg/28,728 lb
Maximum road speed	40 kph/25 mph
Maximum cross-country speed	24 kph/15 mph
Road range	241 km/150 miles
Length	5,791 mm/228 inches
Width	2,502 mm/98.5 inches
Height	2,654 mm/104.5 inches
Engine horse power	150
Track width	357 mm/14 inches
Wheel base	2,210 mm/87 inches
Armament	1 × 2 pdr or 3.7-inch howitzer 3 × 0.303-inch MG
Ammunition carried	100 × 2 pdr 3,000 × 0.303-inch
Armour (overall)	14 mm/0.55 inch
Crew	6

Cruiser Tank Mark II (A10)

The A10 design was produced by Vickers and was basically a more heavily armoured version of the Cruiser Tank Mark I. This was to enable it to be used in an infantry support role but it was often referred to as a 'heavy cruiser'. The new version became the Cruiser Tank Mark II and differed visually from the Mark I in the omission of the two auxiliary turrets of the A9 in favour of a single machine-gun (a 7.92-inch BESA) by the side of the driver. The first Mark II vehicles used the same gun mounting as the Mark I but the Mark IIA featured a revised design. Some 30 Mark IIA vehicles were produced as the Mark IIA CS with a 3.7-inch howitzer. Production ran to 175 tanks by 1940 and these vehicles saw action in France and in Libya where their armour was found to be too light, but the vehicle was preferred to the more unreliable Mark I.

Cruiser Tank Mk ICS, close support version, of the 1st Armoured Division, 1940.

British tank data

Data Cruiser Tank Mark II

Weight in action	14,390 kg/31,696 lb
Maximum road speed	26 kph/16 mph
Maximum cross-country speed	13 kph/8 mph
Road range	161 km/100 miles
Length	5,588 mm/220 inches
Width	2,527 mm/99.5 inches
Height	2,654 mm/104.5 inches
Engine horse power	150
Track width	357 mm/14 inches
Wheel base	2,210 mm/87 inches
Armament	1 × 2 pdr or 3.7-inch howitzer
	2 × 7.92 mm or 0.303-inch MG
Ammunition carried	100 × 2 pdr
	4,050 × 7.92 mm or 0.303-inch
Armour (overall)	30 mm/1.2 inch
Crew	5

Cruiser Tank Mk IIA (A10), 1st Armoured Division, on manoeuvres, 1940.

Cruiser Tank Mark III (A13)

With the design of what was to become the Cruiser Tank Mark III, British tank design undertook a radical step with the adoption of the Christie suspension. This American-designed suspension enabled a tank to have a far higher running speed and an improved cross-country performance with no great increase in engine output, but the early trials with the new A13 design soon produced a large number of troubles that were never entirely eliminated. The Cruiser Mark III was fitted with an American-designed Liberty engine and production was carried out by Nuffields but only 65 were produced. Some of these saw action in France in 1940 and in Libya but in service the type proved unreliable mechanically and was also too lightly armoured for its Cruiser role. Perhaps the most remarkable feature of the A13 design was that it went from the design stage and into service in two years which was a remarkable feat of engineering, but unfortunately the end result was an unsatisfactory tank.

Data Cruiser Tank Mark III

Weight in action	14,237 kg/31,360 lb
Maximum road speed	48 kph/30 mph
Maximum cross-country speed	38 kph/24 mph
Road range	149 km/90 miles
Length	6,020 mm/237 inches
Width	2,540 mm/100 inches
Height	2,591 mm/102 inches
Engine horse power	340
Track width	257 mm/10.125 inches
Wheel base	2,108 mm/83 inches
Armament	1 × 2 pdr
	1 × 0.303-inch MG
Ammunition carried	87 × 2 pdr
	3,750 × 0.303-inch
Armour (overall)	14 mm/0.55 inch
Crew	4

Cruiser Tank Mk III (A13).

Cruiser Tank Mark IV (A13 Mark II)

The Cruiser Tank Mark IV followed the Mark III on the Nuffield production lines in early 1939, and was basically an uparmoured version of the Mark III — the design was originally known as the A13 Mark II. The main visual difference between the two marks was the turret which was much larger on the Mark IV due to the addition of extra 'spaced' armour to the sides. The Cruiser Tank Mark IV became one of the most important British tanks during the early war years and 655 were produced, but in action the Mark IV proved little more successful than the Mark III, mainly due to its general unreliability and the retention of the 2 pdr gun which proved to be too light during the 1940 battles in France and the early Western Desert campaigns — the one good point of the early Christie cruisers was their speed which often got them out of trouble.

The Mark IVA differed from the Mark IV by having a co-axial BESA machine-gun in place of the earlier 0.303-inch Vickers. There was also a Mark IV CS variant. After 1940 many Mark IV tanks were used in the training role.

British tank data

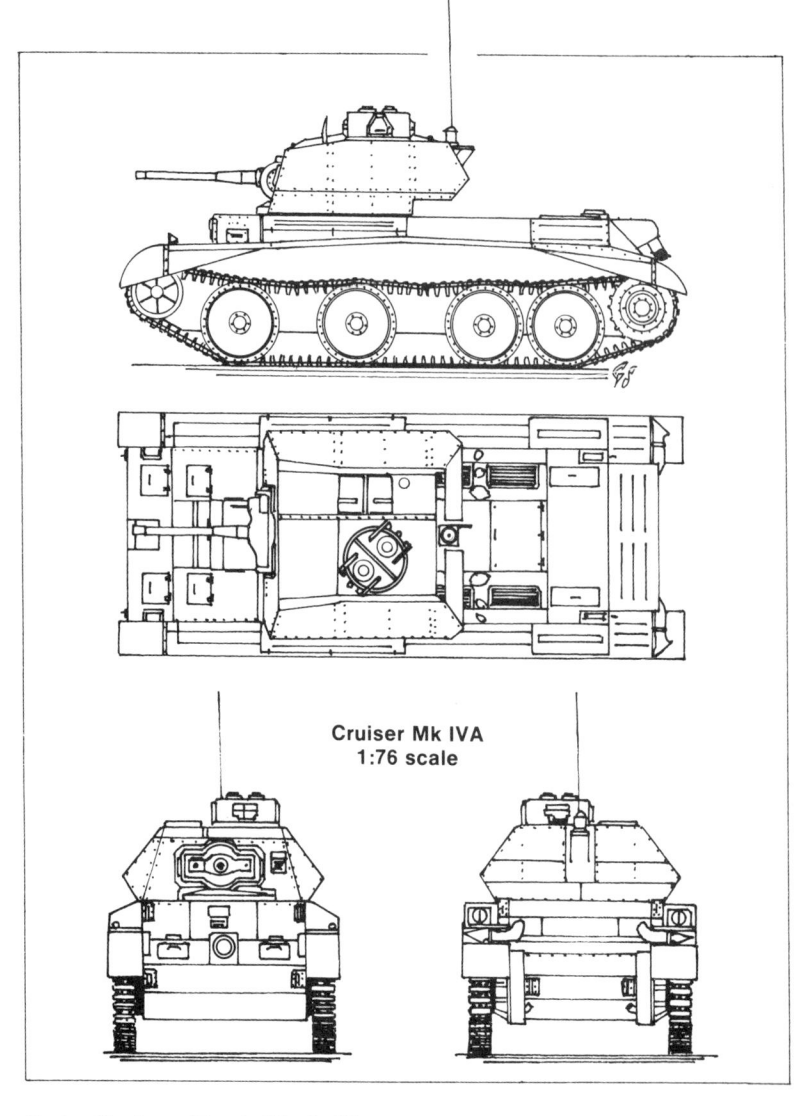

Cruiser Mk IVA
1:76 scale

Data Cruiser Tank Mark IV

Weight in action	15,000 kg/33,040 lb
Maximum road speed	48 kph/30 mph
Maximum cross-country speed	22.5 kph/14 mph
Road range	149 km/90 miles
Length	6,020 mm/237 inches
Width	2,540 mm/100 inches
Height	2,591 mm/102 inches
Engine horse power	340
Track width	257 mm/10.125 inches
Wheel base	2,108 mm/83 inches

British tanks of World War 2

Data Cruiser Tank Mark IV continued

Armament	1 × 2 pdr or 3.7-inch howitzer
	1 × 7.92 mm or 0.303-inch MG
Ammunition carried	87 × 2 pdr
	3,750 × 7.92 mm or 0.303-inch
Armour (overall)	30 mm/1.2 inch
Crew	4

Cruiser Tank Mk IVA with rectangular shaped mantlet and 7.92 Besa machine-gun.

Cruiser Tank Mark V (A13 Mark III)

After the basic A13 and A13 Mark II, the development picture becomes a bit complex as there was an A14 project which came to naught in a welter of mechanical problems, and an A16 which suffered the same fate. Both were cancelled in 1939 and the London Midland and Scottish Railway Company (LMS) were called upon to build a reworked A13 design which had to feature a lower silhouette and 30 mm armour. To decrease the height of the vehicle a 'flat-12' engine was fitted but the radiators necessary for this engine proved to be one of the main causes of the failure of the design as they could not afford the high degree of cooling that the engine required and breakdowns were frequent and endemic. Also the tank was overweight for the suspension which affected the performance. Despite many attempts to cure the engine cooling problems, the Cruiser Tank Mark V, known as Covenanter, never did become an operational tank and its use was confined to the training role, but some were used as bridgelayers, OP tanks, Command tanks, and also as ARV vehicles. The Covenanter tanks ran to four marks which differed only in attempts to improve the cooling problems, and there was the usual CS variant. 1,771 were produced.

Data Covenanter

Weight in action	18,305 kg/40,320 lb
Maximum road speed	50 kph/31 mph
Maximum cross-country speed	40 kph/25 mph
Road range	161 km/100 miles
Length	5,801 mm/228.375 inches
Width	2,610 mm/102.75 inches
Height	2,229 mm/87.75 inches
Engine horse power	280

British tank data

Data Covenanter continued

Track width 273 mm/10.75 inches
Wheel base 2,308 mm/90.875 inches
Armament 1 × 2 pdr or 3-inch howitzer
 1 × 7.92 mm MG
Armour (overall) 40 mm/1.575 inch
Crew 4

Cruiser Tank Mark VI, Crusader (A15)

The Crusader can be regarded as a parallel development of the Covenanter as it was built to a similar specification by Nuffields. Their design designation was A15 and it was a progressive development of the A13 series with Christie suspension (lengthened by an extra road wheel) and retaining the Liberty engine. The first mark retained the 2 pdr gun and had a machine-gun in an auxiliary turret next to the driver but this was eliminated on the next mark in favour of a hull-mounted machine-gun and the third mark was up-gunned to take the first of the 6 pdr guns. The Crusader was produced in some numbers (5,300), and became the most important of all the British tanks that took part in the North African campaigns, but it was no real match for most of the opposing German armour and suffered mainly in its light armour and, initially, the retention of the 2 pdr gun when experience had shown its drawbacks. Also, the Crusader was rushed into service and many mechanical troubles remained 'built in' with the result that the Crusader once more manifested the general unreliability that plagued other British tanks of the period. By mid-1943 the Crusader was withdrawn from service and from then onwards served in a training role, or was converted into a special purpose vehicle, most of which are listed below.

Variants

Crusader I. Initial production model

Cruiser Tank Mk V Covenanter I (A13 Mk III) crossing water obstacle.

Cruiser Tank Mk VI (A15) Crusader I armed with 2 pdr gun. Note auxiliary machine-gun turret that was removed on later models.

with auxiliary turret, often removed once in service.
Crusader II. Version built with hull machine-gun next to driver.
Crusader III. Final production version with 6 pdr gun and increased armour.

Crusader I and II CS. 3-inch howitzer in place of 2 pdr gun.

Crusader OP and Command. Fitted with dummy gun for use as observation post or for general command post with extra radio.

Crusader III, AA Mark I. Normal turret replaced by 40 mm Bofors gun behind shield.

Crusader III, AA Mark II and III. As AA Mark I but with 20 mm twin Oerlikons.

Crusader with triple Oerlikon. A few vehicles were fitted with a special open mount fitted with three Oerlikons.

Crusader II, Gun Tractor Mark I. A special conversion of the Crusader hull for use as a tractor to pull the 17 pdr anti-tank gun. In service 1944-1945.

Crusader ARV.
Crusader Dozer. Turretless version used by Royal Engineers.

Crusader with AMRA Mark Id. Mine clearing device — not used in action.

Crusader III armed with 6 pdr gun in action in Tripolitania, 1943.

British tank data

Data Crusader III

Weight in action	20,085 kg/44,240 lb
Maximum road speed	43 kph/27 mph
Maximum cross-country speed	24 kph/15 mph
Road range (with aux tank)	204 km/127 miles
Length	5,994 mm/236 inches
Width	2,642 mm/104 inches
Height	2,235 mm/88 inches
Engine horse power	340
Track width	273 mm/10.75 inches
Wheel base	2,311 mm/91 inches
Armament	1 × 6 pdr
	1 or 2 × 7.92 mm MG
Ammunition carried	65 × 6 pdr
	5,000 × 7.92 mm
Armour (front)	51 mm/2 inch
Crew	5

Crusader III
1:76 scale

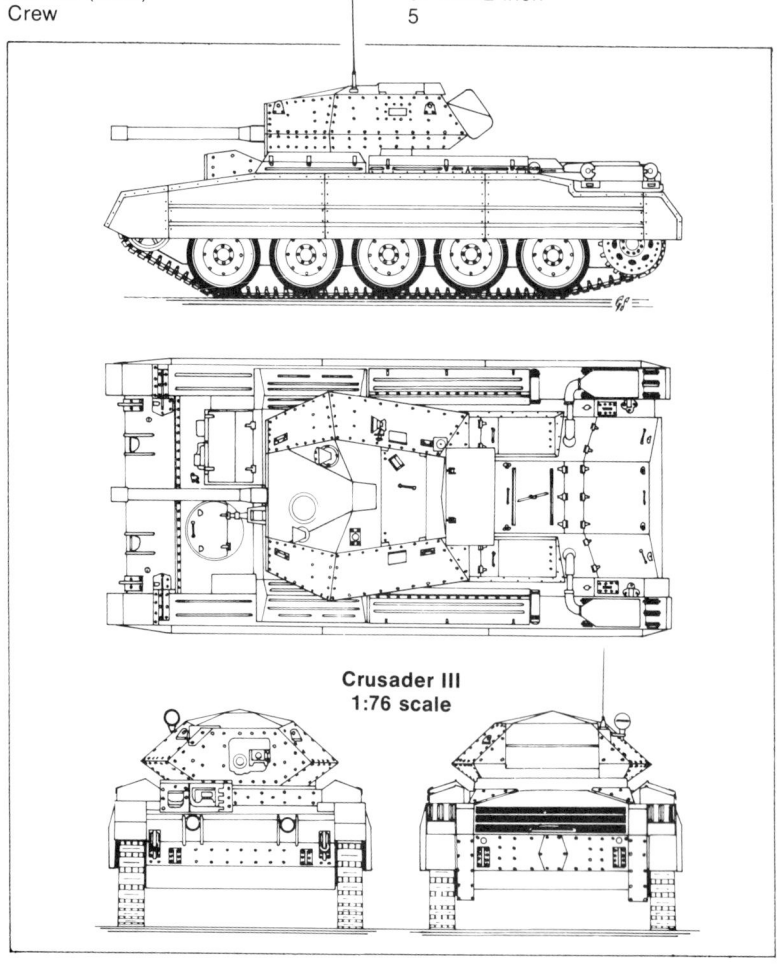

British tanks of World War 2

Crusader II, AA Mk I, developed to protect convoys on the move against low-flying aircraft.

Cruiser Tank Mark VII, Cavalier (A24)

The Crusader performance in battle was closely monitored and the need for a more powerful and heavily armoured tank was soon determined. Design work on what was to become the Cromwell then began (beginning in 1941) but the shortage of suitable engines prevented the rapid introduction of the new design. As a result some 'stop-gap' designs were produced, one of which was the A24, later to be known as the Cavalier. This was basically an up-armoured Crusader and shared the same suspension and Liberty engine. The resultant vehicle, first produced in early 1942, proved to be another unreliable vehicle that had more than its fair share of mechanical troubles, and as a result it never saw first-line service as a gun tank. It was used mainly in the training role, but some were converted to OP tanks and some were converted to ARVs.

Data Cavalier

Weight in action	26,949 kg/59,360 lb
Maximum road speed	39 kph/24 mph
Maximum cross-country speed	22.5 kph/14 mph
Road range	265.5 km/165 miles
Length	6,350 mm/250 inches
Width	2,883 mm/113.5 inches
Height	2,438 mm/96 inches
Engine horse power	410
Track width	356 mm/14 inches
Wheel base	2,467 mm/97.125 inches
Armament	1 × 6 pdr
	1 or 2 × 7.92 MG
Ammunition carried	64 × 6 pdr
	4,950 × 7.92 mm
Armour (frontal)	76 mm/3 inch
Crew	5

British tank data

Cruiser Tank Mark VIII, Centaur (A27L)

The tank that was to become the Cromwell was intended to be powered by the Meteor engine, a derivation of the Rolls-Royce Merlin aircraft engine, but at the time the original A27 design was proposed for production, all Merlin production was earmarked for aircraft use. As an interim solution, it was put forward that the A27 could be fitted with a Liberty engine and converted to the Meteor engine when it became available. The result was known as the A27L, or Centaur, and 950 were produced. Many of these were later converted to full Cromwell configurations, but many Centaurs were used for training, and 80 were fitted with a 95 mm howitzer for use as close support tanks for the beach landings in Normandy. Others were converted as ARVs and AA tanks — a full listing is given below. The first Centaurs were produced in early 1942 and were produced by Leyland Motors.

Centaur IV, 95 mm howitzer assault tank, Royal Marine Armoured Support Regiment, advances into Normandy, 1944.

Variants

Centaur I. First production version fitted with 6 pdr gun.
Centaur III. Fitted with 75 mm gun.
Centaur IV. Fitted with 95 mm howitzer.
Centaur OP. Fitted with dummy gun and extra radios.
Centaur AA Mark I and II. Fitted with twin 20 mm Polsten cannon.
Centaur Kangaroo. A few had their turrets removed to be used as APCs.
Centaur ARV.
Centaur Dozer.

Data Centaur IV

Weight in action	28,874 kg/63,600 lb
Maximum road speed	43 kph/27 mph
Maximum cross-country speed	26 kph/16 mph
Road range	265.5 km/165 miles
Length	6,350 mm/250 inches
Width	2,896 mm/114 inches
Height	2,489 mm/98 inches
Engine horse power	395
Track width	356 mm/14 inches
Wheel base	2,467 mm/97.125 inches
Armament	1 × 95 mm howitzer
	1 or 2 × 7.92 mm MG
Ammunition carried	51 × 95 mm
	4,950 × 7.92 mm
Armour (frontal)	76 mm/3 inch
Crew	5

Cruiser Tank Mark VIII, Cromwell (A27M)

When sufficient Meteor engines became available in early 1943 they were fitted into the A27M, later to be known as the Cromwell. This tank embodied all the lessons learned in

Cromwell IV
1:76 scale

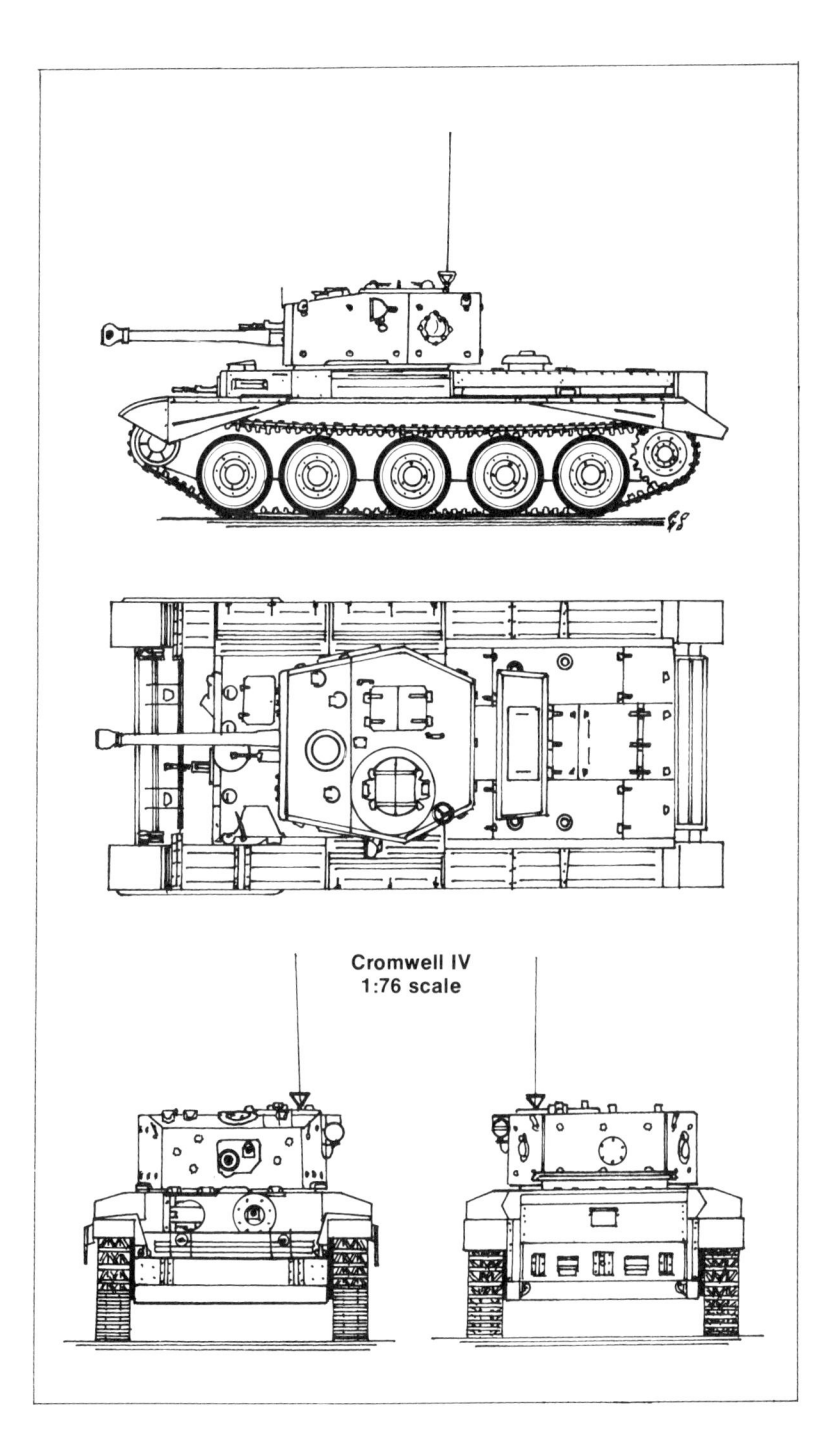

British tank data

such expensive ways during the France and desert campaigns, and as a result it used a tried and tested suspension, good armour and after the first production examples had been fitted with the 6 pdr gun, a new 75 mm gun was fitted. This gun was virtually a scaled-up 6 pdr, but it was not until May 1944 that some early and difficult malfunctions were eliminated. This gun at last put British tanks on some form of parity with German tanks but by the time that the British '75' was in use the Germans were using guns with a longer range and more hitting power. However, the Cromwell was the most important of all the British tanks during 1944 and 1945 both in numbers and quality.

The Cromwell was produced under the parentage of Leyland Motors and remained in production from 1943 until 1945. It was produced in several marks (detailed below) and there were several post-war variants beyond the scope of this book. Many early Cromwells were converted from Centaurs by fitting the Meteor engine.

Variants

Cromwell I. Fitted with 6 pdr gun.
Cromwell II. Fitted with wider tracks and hull machine-gun deleted.
Cromwell III. Originally the Cromwell X, this was a re-engined Centaur I.
Cromwell IV. A re-engined Centaur III.
Cromwell IVw. As Mark IV with an all-welded hull to simplify production.
Cromwell Vw. Similar to Mark IVw.
Cromwell VI. As Mark IV but with 95 mm howitzer.
Cromwell VII. Reworked Cromwell IV with wider tracks, extra armour, suspension modifications and engine changes.
Cromwell VIIw. Cromwell Vw with Cromwell VII changes.
Cromwell VIII. Cromwell VI with Cromwell VII changes.
Cromwell Command or OP. Fitted with dummy gun and extra radios.
Cromwell ARV.
Cromwell CIRD. Mine clearing device — few only.
A33 Assault Tank. Heavy tank for assault role based on Cromwell — prototype only.

Cruiser Tank Mk VIII (A27M) Cromwell IV equipped with 75 mm gun on test trials.

Data Cromwell IV

Weight in action	27,966 kg/61,600 lb
Maximum road speed	51.5 kph/32 mph
Maximum cross-country speed	29 kph/18 mph
Road range	278 km/173 miles
Length	6,350 mm/250 inches
Width	2,908 mm/114.5 inches
Height	2,489 mm/98 inches
Engine horse power	600
Track width	394 mm/15.5 inches
Wheel base	2,467 mm/97.125 inches
Armament	1 × 75 mm
	2 × 7.92 mm MG
Ammunition carried	64 × 75 mm
	4,950 × 7.92 mm
Front armour	63 mm/2.48 inch
Side and rear armour	32 mm/1.26 inch
Turret front armour	76 mm/3 inch
Crew	5

Cruiser Tank, Challenger (A30)

The need for a battle tank to accommodate the 17 pdr anti-tank gun was foreseen as early as 1941, but the tank for which it would have seemed ideal, the Cromwell, was too narrow to mount the size of turret ring necessary to take the extra recoil forces. To provide some form of vehicle to take the 17 pdr, a design study was drawn up with an extended Cromwell chassis with an extra road wheel, a widened centre section, and a new and rather high turret. The Meteor engine was used and Cromwell components were used where possible. The parent company was the Birmingham Carriage and Waggon Co, and production was ordered in early 1943. But production was slow and beset by many troubles. Performance was poor due to the weight involved and some armour had actually to be removed in order to reduce the load; and in March 1944 it was realised that the Challenger had no provision for wading gear and could not therefore take part in the Normandy landings or campaign. By that time the Firefly, a Sherman armed with a 17 pdr, was in widespread use so the Challenger was used in North-West Europe in small numbers only during 1944-1945. 200 were produced.

Data Challenger

Weight in action	33,051 kg/72,800 lb
Maximum road speed	51.5 kph/32 mph
Maximum cross-country speed	24 kph/15 mph
Road range	193 km/120 miles
Length	8,147 mm/320.75 inches
Width	2,908 mm/114.5 inches
Height	2,775 mm/109.25 inches
Engine horse power	600
Track width	394 mm/15.5 inches
Wheel base	2,467 mm/97.125 inches
Armament	1 × 17 pdr
	1 × 0.30-inch Browning MG
Ammunition carried	42 × 17 pdr
Armour (frontal)	101 mm/3.98 inch
Crew	5

Cruiser Tank, Comet (A34)

Almost as soon as the first A27 tanks were coming off the production lines, work was begun on an improved Cromwell which could accommodate a heavier gun. The new design became the A34, later to be called the Comet. Width restrictions prevented the fitting of the normal 17 pdr, but Vickers produced a shorter and lighter version, the 77 mm, which had a performance only marginally lower than the 17 pdr itself and this gun was selected for the Comet. Although it was intended that the Comet would be only an improved Cromwell, the new tank eventually had over 60 per cent new components, including a number

Cruiser Tank, Challenger (A30) in action in Holland, 1944.

of changes to the suspension. The turret was larger also. The first Comets were delivered in December 1944 but that was too late for the type to have any large effect on the course of campaigns in 1945, even though some did see action with the 11th Armoured Division during the Ardennes Offensive of January 1945.

The Comet would have proved itself the best of all the British wartime designs but it came too late in the conflict to make any effect on the course of events, and went on to a long postwar career.

Data Comet

Weight in action	35,775 kg/78,800 lb
Maximum road speed	47 kph/29 mph
Maximum cross-country speed	26 kph/16 mph
Road range	198 km/123 miles
Length	7,652 mm/301.5 inches
Width	3,048 mm/120 inches
Height	2,680 mm/105.5 inches
Engine horse power	600

Comet
1:76 scale

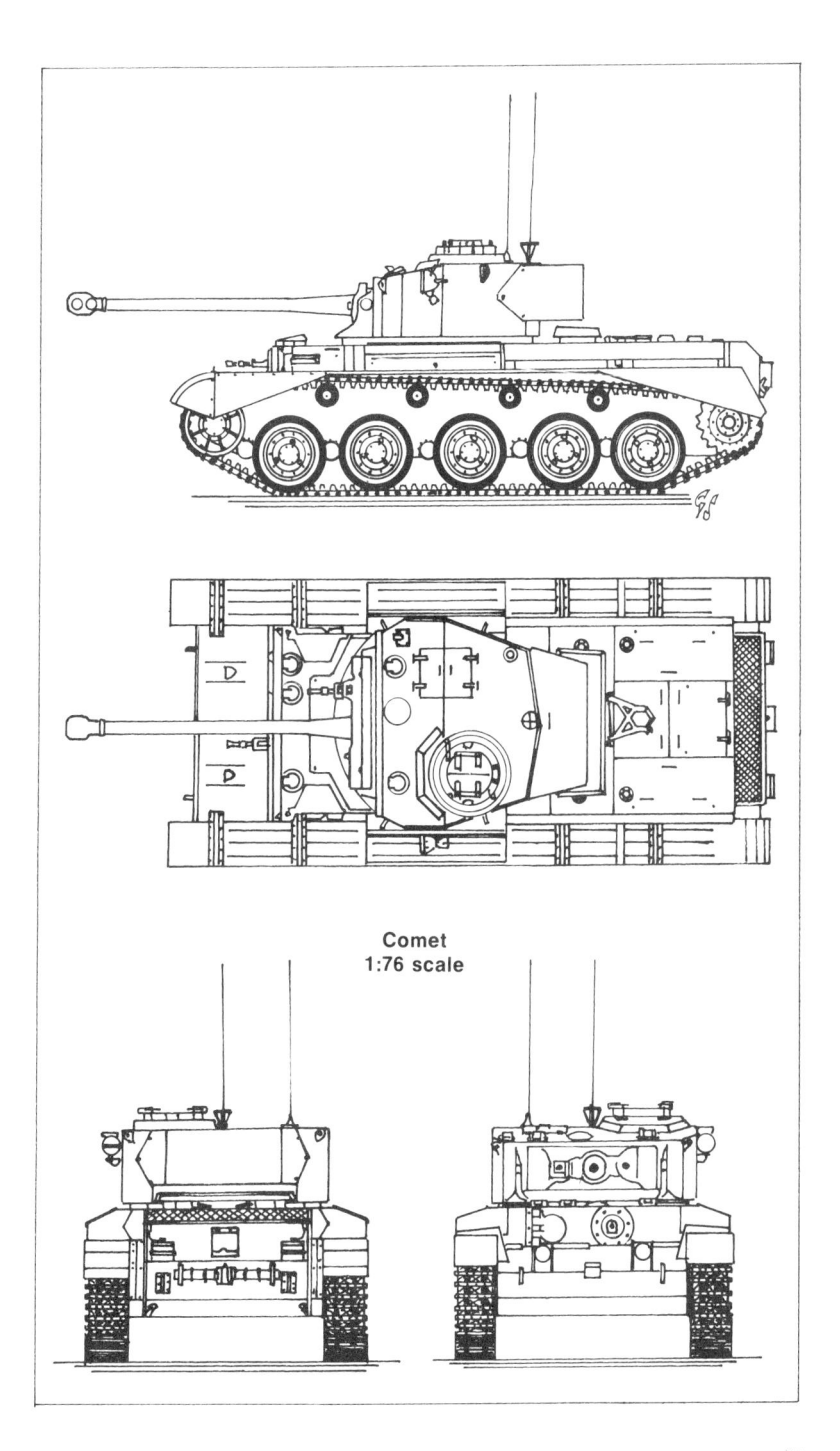

Cruiser Tank, Comet (A34). Gunnery trials on the range, 1944.

Data Comet continued

Track width	394 mm/15.5 inches
Wheel base	2,467 mm/97.125 inches
Armament	1 × 77 mm
	2 × 7.92 mm MG
Ammunition carried	61 × 77 mm
	5,175 mm × 7.92 mm
Front armour	76 mm/3 inch
Side and rear armour	32 mm/1.26 inch
Turret front armour	101 mm/3.98 inch
Crew	5

five

Data on American tanks in British service

The Stuart

Among the very first purchases made from the United States in 1941 was a small batch of M2A4 Light Tanks which were used for training only, but these early purchases were soon replaced by large orders for numbers of the Light Tank, M3, General Stuart. The first Stuart tanks (as they came to be known to the British, although the name Honey was also in use) arrived in the Middle East in July 1941 and thereafter they took part in all the North African and European campaigns. The Stuart was mainly used as a scouting or reconnaissance vehicle but later in the war the turret was often removed to enable the open hull to be used for a variety of purposes. By British standards the Stuart was rather large for a light tank but it gave good and useful service provided it was not expected to be pitted against battle tanks or anti-tank defences. The main British versions are listed below.

Stuart I (M3 Light Tank) on reconnaissance patrol in the Western Desert, 1941.

Variants

Stuart I. M3 with Continental engine.
Stuart II, or Stuart Hybrid. M3 with Guiberson diesel engine.
Stuart III. M3A1 with Continental engine.
Stuart IV or Stuart Hybrid. M3A1 with Guiberson engine.
Stuart V. M3A3.
Turretless Stuarts were used as Kangaroos (APCs), Command tanks, and recce tanks — later many were used as artillery tractors.

Locust light tank (M22) leaving the hold of a Hamilcar glider during training, 1944. Note Airborne badge.

Data Stuart V

Weight in action	14,415 kg/31,752 lb
Maximum road speed	58 kph/36 mph
Maximum cross-country speed	32 kph/20 mph
Road range	112 km/70 miles
Length	5,029 mm/198 inches
Width	2,515 mm/99 inches
Height	2,299 mm/90.5 inches
Engine horse power	250
Track width	295 mm/11.625 inches
Wheel base	1,854 mm/73 inches
Armament	1 × 37 mm
	2 ×0.30-inch Browning MG
Ammunition carried	174 × 37 mm
	6,400 × 0.30-inch
Armour (frontal)	51 mm/2 inch
Crew	4

The Locust

The Light Tank (Airborne) M22 was named the Locust by the British and was used by them in some numbers as a glider-borne tank. The only time it saw action was during the Rhine crossings when a small number were landed from Hamilcar gliders.

Data Locust

Weight in action	7,445 kg/16,400 lb
Maximum road speed	64 kph/40 mph
Maximum cross-country speed	48 kph/30 mph
Road range	217 km/135 miles
Length	3,937 mm/155 inches
Width	2,159 mm /85 inches
Height	1,854 mm/73 inches
Engine horse power	162
Track width	286 mm/11.25 inches
Wheel base	1,791 mm/70.5 inches
Armament	1 × 37 mm
	1 × 0.30-inch MG
Ammunition carried	50 × 37 mm
	2,500 × 0.30-inch
Armour (frontal)	25 mm/0.98 inch
Crew	3

The Lee and Grant

The first of the American 'crash' tank programmes was devoted to producing large numbers of the Medium Tank M3, General Lee. During 1940 a British mission ordered numbers of a version suited to British requirements, and the first were shipped to the Middle East during 1942. These tanks were known to the British as the Grant and differed from the basic M3 in having a redesigned turret with no cupola and a rear overhang to accommodate a radio. The first Grants were bought direct from the makers but after March 1941 the Lease-Lend Act came into being and large numbers were thus supplied by the US Government. Among the Lease-Lend supplies were numbers of the basic M3 series which became known as the Lee to the British.

The main advantage to the British of the Lee and Grant was the sponson-mounted 75 mm gun in the hull. Up till the arrival of the first Grants the British tanks had been consistently

General Lee (Medium Tank M3) in action in the Middle East, 1942.

outgunned by the German tanks and the 75mm gun at last put British tank crews on a parity with their opponents. But the hull mounting restricted the all-important gun traverse so that when sufficient M4 tanks became available the M3s were withdrawn from front line use and converted to special purpose vehicles, or shipped to the Far East where they remained in use until the end of the war. Despite their height and general bulk, the Lee and Grant were in their day the most important tanks in British service and they proved to be good fighting tanks, despite the tactical problems caused by the hull-mounted gun.

Variants

Grant I. The version manufactured to British specifications.
Grant II. American M3A5.
Grant ARV. British conversion of Grant I or II fitted with winches. Some had turret removed.
Grant ARV I. M31 TRV in British use.
Grant Scorpion III and IV. Mine clearing flails driven by extra engine.
Grant CDL. Special turret with searchlight for battlefield illumination.

Data on American tanks in British service

Grant Command. Top turret gun removed for special fitting of radios and map tables.
Lee I. Basic M3 Medium.
Lee II. M3A1.
Lee III. None delivered — would have been M3A2.
Lee IV. M3A3.
Lee V. M3A3 fitted with diesel engine.
Lee VI. M3A4.

105 mm SP, Priest.

Data Grant

Weight	27,240 kg/60,000 lb
Maximum road speed	42 kph/26 mph
Maximum cross-country speed	25 kph/16 mph
Road range	193 km/120 miles
Length	5,639 mm/222 inches
Width	2,718 mm/107 inches
Height	2,845 mm/112 inches
Engine horse power	340
Track width	419 mm/16.5 inches
Wheel base	2,108 mm/83 inches
Armament	1 × 75 mm
	1 × 37 mm
	3 or 4 × 0.30-inch MG
Ammunition carried	46 × 75 mm
	178 × 37 mm
	9,200 × 0.30-inch
Front armour	51 mm/2 inch
Side armour	38 mm/1.5 inch
Rear armour	38 mm/1.5 inch
Turret front armour	57 mm/2.25 inch
Crew	6

105 mm SP, Priest

Although not strictly speaking a tank, the Priest was an important addition to the British armoury when the first deliveries were made in late 1942. At that time the British tank formations had to rely on towed artillery for fire support and the Priest, with its 105 mm howitzer, gave the artillery the ability to be fully mobile and keep up with the tanks. The Priest was the Howitzer Motor Carriage M7, built on to the chassis of the M3 tank. It served throughout the desert and Italian campaigns, but its calibre of 105 mm was a drawback in the standardisation of ammunition, and when enough 25 pdr-equipped Sextons became available the Priest was withdrawn and used, minus the howitzer, as a Kangaroo APC or OP vehicle. Despite its open fighting compartment the Priest was a popular and efficient vehicle, and served on until the early Normandy battles.

The Sherman

The most important Allied tank of World War 2, outside Russia, was undoubtedly the Sherman. By sheer numbers alone it featured as one of the most important 'war winners' of that conflict and after the beginning of 1943 it became the most important single item in the British armoured formations. Huge numbers of Shermans were supplied to the British on Lease-Lend terms, and there were very many different versions delivered. The

British tanks of World War 2

full story of the Sherman will be told in a future Airfix Guide and this volume can only deal with the 'British' versions.

The Sherman (officially General Sherman) was the Medium Tank M4 Sherman. The first urgent deliveries were made to the Middle East in October 1942 — these were the M4A1 variant, and they took part in the El Alamein battle. Thereafter the numbers and variants multiplied and every improvement made on the American production lines was at some time or other reflected in the models supplied to the British. The one big exception was the M4A3 which was 'standardised' as the main American tank for their own tank divisions. Thus in British service could be seen vehicles with cast or welded hulls, differing suspensions and armaments ranging from 75 mm and 76 mm guns to 105 mm howitzers. The main listing of variants is given below.

However, there were two main British variations — the DD tanks and the Firefly. The DD tanks were 'swimming' tanks that floated ashore from landing craft. Their buoyancy came from canvas screens fitted round the hull sides. Once ashore the screens could be discarded and the main armament brought into play. The DD (Duplex Drive) tanks were used during the Normandy landings and subsequent river crossings, and the Sherman was the type selected as the 'standard' tank for this purpose.

The Firefly was a Sherman fitted with a 17 pdr gun. Its early development life was rather uncertain as the British Challenger was intended to be the main 17 pdr tank, but development of this tank was very slow and full of difficulty so the Sherman variant was selected as a 'back-up' project. In February 1944 it became obvious that the Challenger would not be available in sufficient numbers so the Sherman project, named Firefly, went ahead. By June 1944 there were only enough to be issued at the rate of one per troop, but as it was the only Allied tank able to take on the German Panthers on anything like equal terms, it was a very important fighting vehicle. In time more became available and the type served on until the end of the war in Europe. Most Firefly conversions were made on M4A4 chassis (Firefly VC). On all conversions the hull machine-gun was removed for extra ammunition stowage.

Sherman Firefly VC (Medium Tank M4A4) and Sherman Vs of the 2nd Armoured Irish Guards crossing Nijmegen bridge.

Data on American tanks in British service 53

Despite its numerical importance the Sherman was not a very good fighting tank. It was high and rather lightly armoured, and its armament tended to lag behind German advances. But all this was made up for by sheer numbers — there were more Shermans in British service than all other types put together.

Variants

Sherman I. Basic M4.
Sherman Hybrid I. Late production M4.
Sherman IB. M4 with 105 mm gun.
Sherman IBY. Late M4 with 105 mm gun — late 1945.
Sherman II. M4A1 (cast hull).
Sherman IIA. M4A1 with 76 mm gun.
Sherman IIC (Firefly). M4A1 with 17 pdr gun.
Sherman III. M4A2.
Sherman IIIAY. Late production M4A2.
Sherman IV. M4A3 — few delivered.
Sherman IVA. Late production M4A3.
Sherman IVB. M4A3 with 105 mm gun.
Sherman IVC (Firefly). M4A3 with 17 pdr gun.
Sherman V. M4A4.

Sherman Tankdozer, normal Sherman tank fitted with dozer blade for levelling steep banks, clearing blockages, etc.

Sherman VC (Firefly). Main version with 17 pdr gun — M4A4.
Sherman (Tulip). Sherman V fitted with rocket launchers on turret sides, Normandy 1944.
Sherman ARV. ARV conversions to Sherman III and V. Sherman II ARV Mark III was US M32B1 TRV.
Sherman BARV. Converted ARV with added superstructure for deep wading on beaches.

Sherman Crab II, fitted with flail for detonating mines.

Sherman Kangaroo. Turretless APC to carry ten men into action.
Sherman Gun Tower. Used to tow 17 pdr anti-tank gun in Italy.
Sherman OP/Command. Extra radios fitted — some had dummy gun. Also a Rear Link version.
Sherman Plymouth. Bailey Bridge carrier with no turret. Used in Italy.

Mine Clearing devices: Scorpion IV; Marquis; Lobster; Crab — I and II; CIRD; AMRCR; and Centipede.
Flamethrowers: Adder; Salamander; and Badger.

As well as the above there were many other experimental versions that never saw action and are thus outside the scope of this book.

Data Sherman III

Weight in action	31,326 kg/69,000 lb
Maximum road speed	39 kph/24 mph
Maximum cross-country speed	24 kph/15 mph
Road range	160-240 km/100-150 miles
Length	5,893 mm/232 inches
Width	2,616 mm/103 inches
Height	2,743 mm/108 inches
Engine horse power	375
Track width	419 mm/16.5 inches
Wheel base	2,108 mm/83 inches
Armament	1 × 75 mm gun
	2 × .30-inch MG
	1 × .50-inch MG (optional)
Ammunition carried	97 × 75 mm
	4,750 × .30 inch
Front armour	51 mm/2 inch
Side armour	51 mm/2 inch
Rear armour	38 mm/1.5 inch
Turret front armour	76 mm/3 inch
Crew	5

SP 25 pdr Sexton. Used by British Artillery in a support role. Basic chassis Ram II tank.

Data on American tanks in British service

Wolverine and Achilles

The Wolverine was originally an M4A2 hull fitted with an open-topped turret, and known as the Gun Motor Carriage M10. The gun was a 3-inch anti-tank gun and the M10 was intended to be a mobile tank destroyer. This version was known to the British as the 3-inch SP, Wolverine, and some were delivered in 1944. Once in British hands the gun was often replaced by a 17 pdr so that

Anti-tank SP 17 pdr M10 (Achilles). This was the British 17 pdr Anti-tank gun mounted on the Sherman chassis.

the name then became 17 pdr SP, Achilles Mark IC. (The Mark IIC was converted from the later M10A1). With either gun the vehicle was a well-armed and successful tank-killer that saw action in Europe until the end of hostilities.

six

British tank armament

As a general rule, British tank armament lagged behind other nations in many respects. The main reasons for this state of affairs are complex but can be said to have originated in 1935 when the 2 pdr gun was selected as the main armament of the British tank arm. This gun had a calibre of 40 mm and at the time of its selection it was as good as any other gun then in existence, but by 1940 this state of affairs no longer applied. German tanks went into action in France in 1940 armed with 75 mm guns which had a much greater armour penetration at ranges in excess of the 2 pdr, and these German tanks had armour that the 2 pdr could not penetrate at combat ranges. The 2 pdr was also unable to fire a HE round which led to the fitting of 3-inch and 3.7-inch howitzers to special CS close support tanks, but the main problem of the 2 pdr was its effect on British tank design. With the choice of the 2 pdr as the main tank armament for some years to come the size of the turret ring was fixed, and with this the width of the tank hull was also fixed. When the time came to select a heavier gun to replace the 2 pdr, the size of the new gun was restricted by the small size of the turret ring. When a tank gun is fired the recoil forces are spread round the diameter of the turret ring and the heavier the gun, the larger the ring diameter has to be. After 1940, when the need for heavier tank guns was realised, only a relatively small increase in gun calibre could be made as the tank widths could not accommodate larger turret rings. Thus a new range of tank designs had to be produced which meant delays, expense and facilities being consumed to the detriment of production.

With the eclipse of the 2 pdr, the next gun to be placed into production was the 57 mm 6 pdr. This weapon had a much better performance than the 2 pdr but by the time it reached the field it was already obsolescent as by 1942 the German tanks were armed with the 'long' 75 mm gun and the 88 mm gun was in the offing. Russian tanks were in action with a 76 mm gun well before the 6 pdr saw widespread service. Thus the 6 pdr can be regarded as a 'stop-gap' weapon only, pending the next generation of tank designs to carry heavier calibres. As far as the tank crews were concerned, the day was saved by the arrival in the field of the American 75 mm gun fitted to the Lee/Grant and Sherman. This gun enabled British tank crews to fight German armour on a more equal basis but even as this gun became available in quantity, the German designers were producing the L/70 75 mm gun fitted to the Panther and the 88 mm gun-armed Tiger was in service. But the American 75 mm gun was a good all-round weapon and was available in large numbers. It was also put into production in the UK, but the British 'answer' to the tank armament problem was the 76.2 mm 17 pdr. This large gun at last enabled the British tanks to fight on a parity with German tanks but due to its large recoil forces a new tank design was again necessary, and the gun saw action in quantity when fitted to the Firefly. A derivative of the 17 pdr, known as the 77 mm, was produced for the Comet. This variant had a performance only slightly lower than the normal 17 pdr.

All the British tanks used during World War 2 were fitted with at least one machine-gun. Up till 1940 most of these machine-guns were the bulky, water-cooled Vickers .303-inch guns, but the larger .5-inch Vickers gun was used as the main armament of the Light Tanks and the Matilda I. By 1940 the notion of using a machine-gun as the main tank weapon was dropped and thereafter the machine-gun was used as a co-axial weapon mounted alongside the main armament with another gun mounted in the hull front. After 1939, a Czech 7.92 mm gun, manufactured in the UK as the Besa, replaced the Vickers gun as the standard tank machine-gun. This gun was air-cooled and belt fed, and was a much more compact and handy weapon. Many tanks also carried a roof-mounted Bren gun for AA defence, but this gun could be easily dismounted for use as a normal light machine-gun in local defence. A heavy 15 mm Besa machine-gun was produced in small numbers but was fitted only to the Light Tank Mark VIC

Tank gun data

	2 pdr	6 pdr	75 mm (M2)	17 pdr	77 mm
Calibre	40 mm	57 mm	75 mm	76.2 mm	76.2 mm
Muzzle velocity	2,800 ft/sec	2,800 ft/sec	1,860 ft/sec	1,885 ft/sec	2,600 ft/sec
Shot weight (AP)	1.375 lb	6.25 lb	14.92 lb	17 lb	17 lb
Armour penetration (at 500 yards/ 30°)	57 mm	81 mm	60 mm	120 mm	109 mm

seven

Camouflage and markings

Camouflage

The earliest British tanks were not camouflaged at all but were painted in a dark Admiralty grey as befitted their concept as 'land battleships'. Once the element of surprise had been lost, attempts were made at camouflage by the application of green and brown paint in irregular patterns, helped by the layers of battlefield mud. The tanks which followed the initial group were clad in a brownish shade of khaki and this scheme was to persist until the 1930s. The khaki scheme was then replaced by a semi-matt dark green, and this was still to be seen after September 1939. On that date there were three main paint schemes in use:

Pre-war dark green. Mostly confined to non-operational units such as training schools, but also used on most vehicles produced pre-1939 in service in Malaya and Hong Kong, and in temperate areas of India.

A *Sherman Mark 1 of 13th/18th Hussars, 27th Armoured Brigade. Khaki overall, yellow turret top and 'diamond' on side. White 12, black panel forward of diamond with 'TWELFTH KNIGHT' in red thereon. K313 in white on right front above the tracks, and 27th Armoured Brigade's white/gold seahorse on a blue shield on left front.*

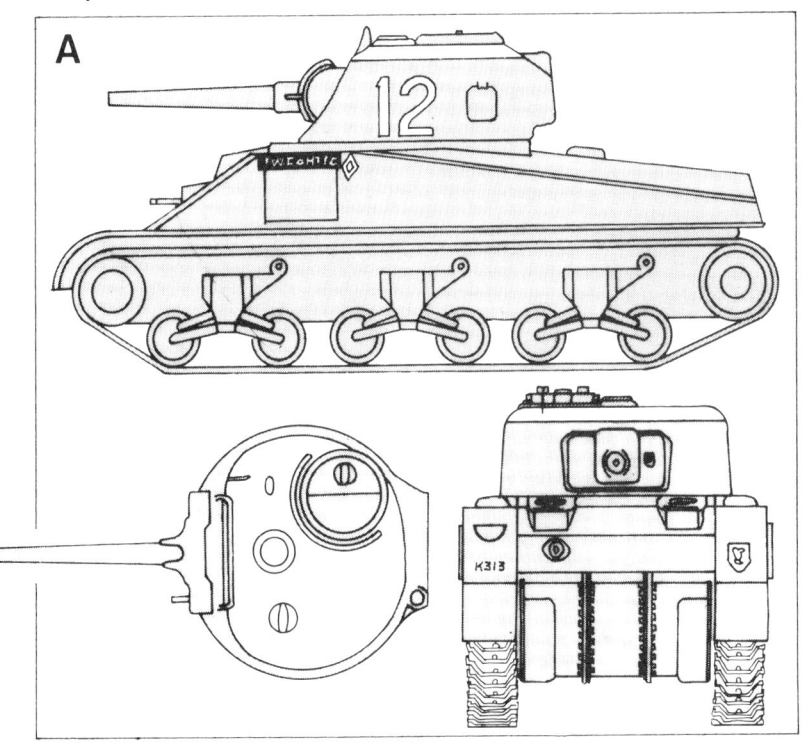

Camouflage and markings

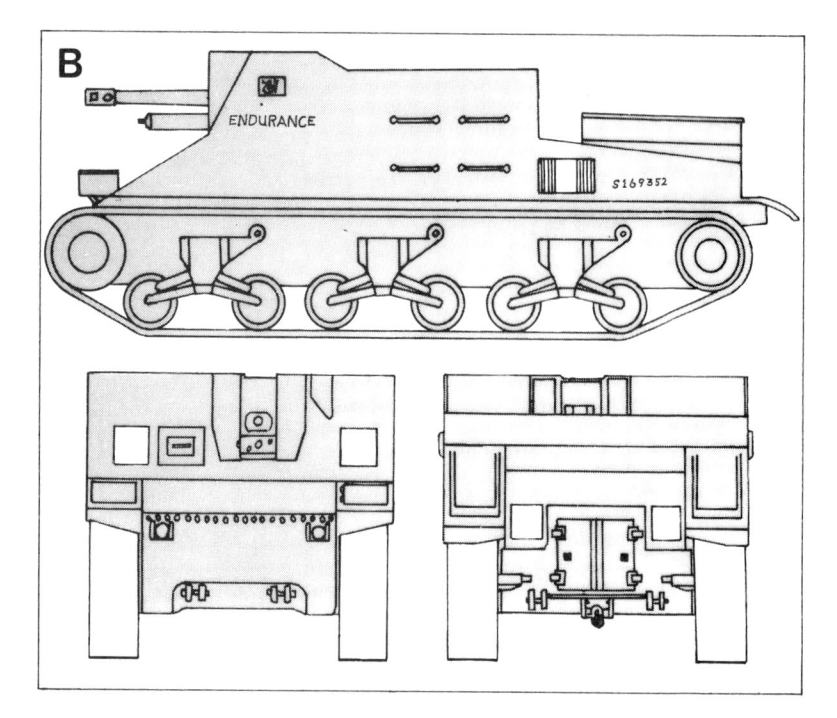

Khaki. Of a more greenish tone than the previous shade and matt in finish. This scheme was used on most operational AFVs serving in Europe and the UK, and was the 'production' finish for all new vehicles.

Sand. Another matt finish, favoured in the Middle East and hot dry areas of India.

Exceptions did exist where vehicles were rapidly transferred as emergency reinforcements, and new vehicles arrived in areas where khaki was not in common use; whether or not they were repainted depended on local paint stocks.

Europe 1939-42

Although the khaki finish was basic for all AFVs in this theatre, it served only as a casual concealment and several disruptive schemese were tried by overpainting in various colours. The objective being to break up the outline of a vehicle, the colours used were dark in contrast to the 'light' khaki. Two main schemes were used:

B *Sexton. Overall khaki. Side view shows location of RAC flash on an Italian-based Sexton, with the name 'Endurance' below the gun breech on the port side, midway down, and serial S169352 below the rear stowage boxes, both yellowish. Back and front views show the location of unit and formation signs.*

Dark green/khaki. Principally used until the end of 1940, but except for the BEF was rarely seen on tanks.

Black/khaki. Introduced towards the end of 1940 to supersede the earlier scheme. The black weathered to a dark grey — where only a thin coat had been applied, to a dark brownish shade.

Both schemes were applied in the style of RAF aircraft camouflage, ie irregular stripes and patches with a wavy outline over the basic khaki.

Middle East 1939-43

The basic finish for AFVs in this

C

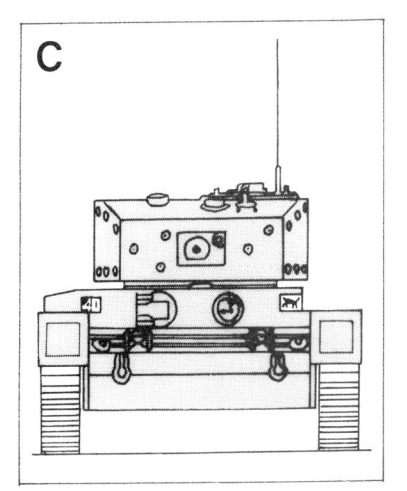

C *Cromwell*. This is a command tank of 11th Armoured Division (black bull on yellow oblong) bearing the name 'Tuareg 11' above the divisional sign and the serial T187816 centrally between the ring bolts on the hull front, both in white. The bridging number 80 is in black on the overall khaki outlined by a thin yellow ring placed to left of serial. The white number 40 on the right front is on black.

theatre was the overall sand colour already in use, and was applied to most new arrivals before action. This applied to British, Commonwealth and Allied (French, Polish, Greek) formations, and varied in tint from a yellowish cream to a pinky-brown shade depending on the paint stocks used and the degree of weathering. From 1940 onwards camouflage patterns were applied over this basic finish. Two main schemes were employed:

1940-41. A 'splinter' camouflage of matt light blue and matt black applied in fan-like patterns, ie either parallel wedges, or divergent wedges. The blue varied from pale blue to bluish-grey. The black was often applied so thinly that a dark brown effect was created — applied more thinly, it soon weathered to a grey.

1941-43. A Home Forces RAF style was used, the stripes and patches being mainly matt black or earth, although a matt dark green was occasionally used. These colours weathered to dark grey, dark brown and medium green.

Both schemes were subjected to a considerable degree of interpretation, so that vehicles in the same unit were often not exactly alike in finish. Sometimes the top of a tank would be left in the original sand finish.

Because of the open nature of the terrain and the need for concealment of armour on the move, tanks were occasionally fitted with a canvas tilt simulating the cab and body of a truck. On Crusaders the centre three road wheels were 'blacked-out' to give a distant impression of a four-wheeled truck. This type of 'camouflage' was unique to the 8th Army.

The Malta garrison developed a unique local camouflage. Over the basic sand finish a 'crazy paving' pattern of lines in dark earth was applied, effectively breaking up the outline of the vehicle.

Far East 1939-42

No special finish was used in the Far East theatre during this period. Starting with the basic schemes outlined earlier in 1939, two further schemes were later in use. First came the standard Home Service khaki on new production vehicles, and later came US Army olive drab on new AFVs supplied direct to this theatre.

Europe 1942-45

Towards the end of 1942 a new scheme was introduced for use in Europe and temperate climates. Another shade of khaki was introduced with a distinct reddish-brown tinge. Over this finish was applied the famous 'Mickey Mouse ear' scheme: basically irregular patches formed by a grouping of discs of varying diameters, painted in matt black in intensities varying from thin (giving dark brown) to solid. Additionally, the horizontal surfaces could be painted matt black. Few AFVs used the full scheme; most

Camouflage and markings 61

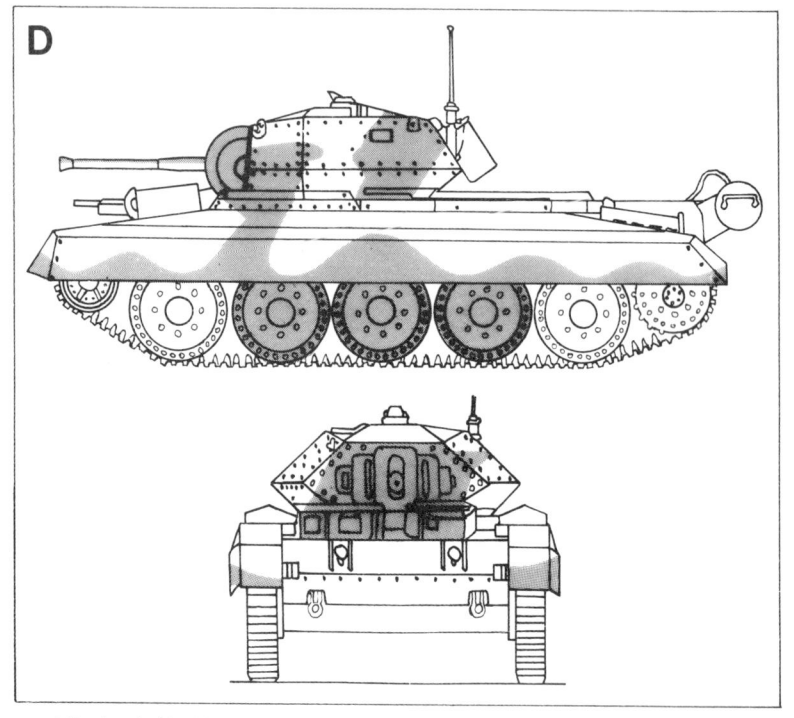

D *Crusader. Western Desert sand/dark grey scheme.*

used the basic khaki scheme only, and occasionally turret tops were painted matt black.

For the Normandy landings, Sherman BARVs and armoured bulldozers were painted in light Admiralty grey. A white finish was applied locally in the winter Ardennes campaign of 1944-45.

Far East 1942-45

Form 1942 onwards a dark dull brown was used on vehicles built in India and Australia. This was mainly used on soft-skinned vehicles, but a small number of AFVs did appear in this finish. Equally small in number were the vehicles in the 'Mickey Mouse ear' finish mentioned above. The vast majority appear to have been in overall khaki (1939 shade) or US olive drab, both weathered by local conditions.

Markings

The earliest form of recognition marking on British tanks was the device known as the 'RAC flash'. During World War 1, the need arose to identify British tanks from German (German A7Vs and captured British). A white stripe with a central red stripe was painted on the front side plates; further variations followed but the colours and divisions remained the same. This device was re-adopted in 1939 in reversed colours, ie red/white/red, and was widely used by units in France, the UK and North Africa until 1942. After this date its use declined with the introduction of the Allied white star recognition symbol, although it was still to be seen in Italy as late as 1944, and also on specialised vehicles such as OP tanks and SP artillery, up to 1945. Occasionally the RAC flash was used in the old 1914-18 style, ie white/red/white; as far as can be traced this was unique to Royal Tank Regiments units in the 8th Army, 1941-42.

British tanks of World War 2

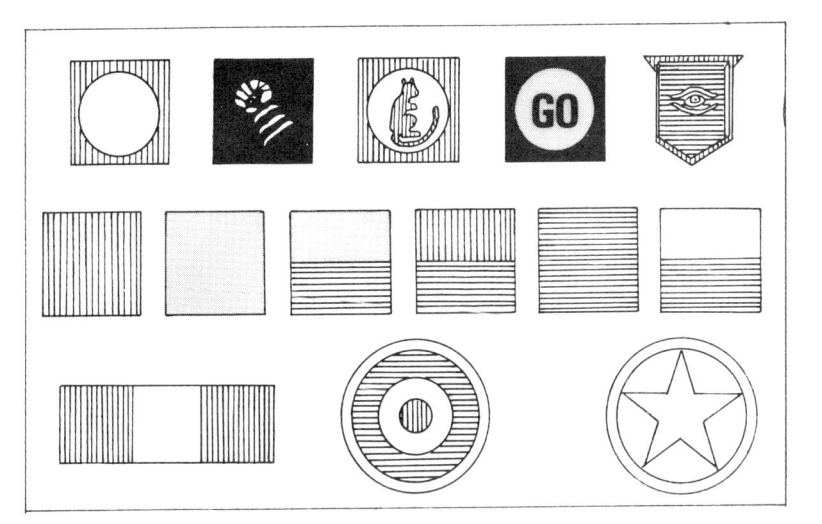

Formation and Identification signs

Top line *(let to right)* Mobile Division 1940 *(red square, white circle)*; 6th Armoured Division *(white fist on black)*; 7th Armoured Division *(red rat and square on white)*; 8th Armoured Division *(black 'GO' and square, green circle)*; Guards Armoured Division *(white eye, blue shield, red border)*. **Middle line** Senior Armoured Brigade *(red)*; Junior Armoured Brigade *(green)*; Reconnaissance regiment *(green over blue)*; Artillery regiment *(red over blue)*; Engineer squadrons *(blue)*; Divisional signals *(white over blue)*; All numerals white except divisional signals *(red)*. **Bottom line** RAC flash; First style aircraft recognition sign — red / white / blue / yellow from inside outwards; Second style aircraft recognition sign — to be seen with or without broken ring.

The white star marking used to identify US Army vehicles was generally adopted in early 1944 as the standard air-recognition marking for all Allied military vehicles. Prior to this, it had been customary to paint the appropriate air force roundel on turret tops or engine covers to identify 'friendly' armour. The star marking was applied, with and without a stencilled 'broken ring' surround on turret tops, frontal and side armour; rarely in all locations but always in at least one.

Further recognition markings were used for specific operations — a light colour (possibly yellow) was applied to the tops of Shermans of the 13th/18th Hussars in 1944, extending over the whole top but not the sides (coincidentally, no star marking was visible).

Regimental and squadron markings

The means of identification within a division or brigade was complex. It should not have been so but for the rapid expansion of the armoured forces in the late 1930s. During the early 1930s a system of battalion or regiment identification within the division, and squadron identification within regiments, was in use which employed the colour and shape of symbols. Thus the senior regiment/battalion had red symbols, with yellow, blue and green for the next three regiments/battalions in order of seniority. The symbols were as follows: 'A' Squadron — hollow triangle, point upwards; 'B' Squadron — hollow square; 'C' Squadron — hollow circle; 'D' Squadron — vertical

Camouflage and markings

oblong stripe; HQ Squadron — hollow diamond.

The above is the official interpretation of the scheme. In practice, the regimental colours were often used to identify squadrons; others used different colours — eg 5th RTR, 1st Armoured Division, used purple signs when in France 1939-40. A further embellishment was added with numbers within the symbol to identify tanks within troops: this was regularised during 1943-44 with the introduction of new wireless procedures when tanks were designated within troops. As an example, a number identified the troop and a number the individual tank — thus 3A would be the first tank (probably the troop leader's) in No 3 troop. These codes were often placed within the squadron symbol.

The geometric symbol usually appeared on hull or turret sides, in conformity with all other Army vehicles. Tanks were required to carry regimental identity marks facing front and rear. This mark took the form of a coloured rectangle with a two-digit number painted on it. By this time, armour was organised in armoured brigades within divisions, usually of three regiments/battalions. The senior brigade had red rectangles, the junior green, and each regiment was identified by a unique number. The reconnaissance regiment of each division was identified by a two-colour square split horizontally, normally green over blue, although some 8th Army units are known to have used green over white. Other arms using AFVs were the Royal Engineers (blue rectangle), Royal Signals (white over blue), and the Royal Artillery (red over blue). In most case numerals were white: exceptions were the Royal Signals (red) and the green/white 8th Army recce units (black).

Names were frequently painted on tanks. In general they followed a regimental scheme. Most used a squadron letter, eg when 'A' Squadron had names all starting with 'A'. The smaller and more independent the unit, the greater was the occurrence of 'freestyle' naming.

Divisional markings

These were first formulated during 1917 and 1918 and the same rules seem to have been applied to World War 2 divisional signs, ie regional symbols, stylised initials and allusions to the divisional role. Thus 7th Armoured Division, raised in the desert, chose the jerboa (the Desert Rat) as their symbol. 1st Armoured Division chose the rhino, and the 6th Armoured Division chose the mailed fist, both indicative of their armoured role.

Further reading on camouflage markings

British Military Markings 1939-45, by P. Hodges. (Almark).
Armour Camouflage & Markings, North Africa 1940-1943, by G. Bradford. (Arms & Armour Press).
British & Commonwealth Armoured Formations (1919-45), by D. Crow. (Profile Publications).